Elliott O'Connor. R
Graham assisted with creatin
I recently married and had the fear i
proposed. I am not a natural public sp
a true reflection of the steps I took witl
confidence to deliver the speech that I had become so proud of. If you want
to impress your guests, your wife and more importantly yourself with a
memorable speech...
then this is the book for you.

Terri Shanks. Marriage & Funeral Celebrant—
Founder & Director of The Fellowship of Professional Celebrants.
I am an experienced public speaker myself and yet still learnt some new and
very relevant tips from reading this book, so whether you are an experienced
speaker or complete novice I would highly recommend this book to anyone as
an enlightening and informative read.

Tony Winyard. Award-Winning
Master of Ceremonies and Wedding DJ.
Having been at over 2,000 weddings and witnessed thousands of wedding
speeches I would thoroughly recommend the advice delivered by Graham. I
love the way it's been crafted into a fascinating story with easy, actionable tools
and easy to remember acronyms... An excellent book with sound suggestions
that is sure to enable you to confidently deliver a superb wedding speech.

John Hope. Proprietor at The Priory, Little Wymondley, Hertfordshire—
Award-Winning Wedding Venue.
When it comes to the art and practice of making the perfect wedding speech
Graham Le-Gall is the master. In this book he delineates humorously, in the
words of his alter ego Reg, to his student Ashley—the groom to be—how to
make the speech of his life. Reg calls the elements that have to come together
to make a perfect wedding speech his 'peas'. Skilfully he weaves his narrative to
incorporate the stages that build to the climax, the delivery on the day of the
wedding. I can speak with some authority on the effectiveness of Graham's
tuition because some years ago he guided me through the process to a minor
triumph on the big day and no student needed more support and guidance
than I. And because not every potential student can sit at the feet of the
master this little volume amply fills that gap.

Alex Bell FRSA. Leadership coach and creator of
'exciting, inspirational' learning events globally.
Graham Le-Gall has produced a really well structured, engaging and truly
entertaining how-to guide to arguably the most important landmark speech of
our lives. Follow his advice and you're in safe hands for your big day.

Beatrice Holloway. Author.
The reader is led on step by step with sound advice, and at the end of most chapters is a very detailed bonus (Reg's pea-pod) that emphasises each point towards the perfection of a speech. Another bonus is the comic pictures that illustrate the points raised.
… I found the book informative, charming.

Tony Lampert. Father of the bride in 11 days! Aaaarrrgghhh…
An essential and entertaining four-hour read for the unprepared, unfocused and unstructured, reluctant wedding speaker.

Keith Martin. Father of four sons—
four Father of the Groom speeches.
I wish I'd read it before my last effort!

Pat Tuohy. Recent Father of the Bride.
This book was the process myself and the Groom followed, all I can personally say it was invaluable as our speeches, including the Peas, went down a storm. I have a family friend who is going to be the Groom later this year and will definitely be recommending that he reads this book.

John Constable. Graham's Best Man over 40 years ago.
Just finished it—fantastic! I wish this book was available decades ago when I first made an effort of a best man speech, I have been best man now four times and really wish this book of knowledge was available then. It is very informative with the tips and skills needed to make a memorable wedding speech backed up with some great drawings.
It gives the reader confidence and hints to make either a great groom or best man speech. Highly recommend it.

G. Riley Mills. Author of The Bullseye Principle—Mastering Intention-Based Communication to Collaborate, Execute, and Succeed.
Filled with useful information and easy-to-apply tips, this book is perfect for the reluctant wedding speaker who wants to deliver a speech that people will be talking about for years.

Emma Mitchell. Decadent Diamonds—Your Private Jeweller.
What a fantastic book! I have already had friends asking me for pointers from it! An interesting and educational read told within an enchanted and relatable story. A must read for any public-speaking-phobes.

Lulu Dale. Trainer & Examiner of Public Speaking—
Soon to be Mother of the Bride.
I really enjoyed the book, it was an easy read and the story telling was compelling… By the end, the methodical approach… made me feel that even I could come up with a speech if so required!

HOW TO MAKE A
CONFIDENT AND
MEMORABLE
WEDDING SPEECH

THE PEAS OF PUBLIC SPEAKING

Graham Le-Gall

Illustrated by Les Ellis

 mPowr

mPowr Publishing Presents...

When you pick up a book by mPowr Publishing you are in for an adventure. Our passion is transformational content, ideas, stories, tools and strategies that empower lives, businesses and communities. You are not likely to get what you expect but you will always find what you need. We don't do bland, generic information. We celebrate the inner quirk, the outer quest and the joy of building legacies that last! Adventurers, Be Enchanted!

Contents

To my wife and friend - Jenny.

Introduction

It is likely that you haven't had too much experience in public speaking. Most people called to speak at a wedding are not veterans in standing up in front of an audience and their inexperience can cause a lot of anxiety and fear. Many people in this situation bury their heads in the sand until it is too late. This leads to speeches that leave a lot to be desired and which are remembered for the wrong reasons.

If you want to feel comfortable and confident about speaking at a wedding, this book is for you. Whether you are the bride, groom, best person or have some other speaking role, you will discover how to create a speech that is memorable for all the right reasons.

This book is different. I don't think you will find another book about wedding speeches quite like it.

Oftentimes, the stories told at a wedding are the ones that make the biggest impact and are remembered long after the event has passed.

This is why this book has been designed around a story. The familiar tale of two young people who meet, fall in love and decide to get married. And then, the lesser-known story about the preparations for the wedding, in which some family and friends—like you and yours—are busy organising the wedding and thinking about their speeches. And the tale of those who do all that they can to avoid thinking about speech preparation.

You will be introduced to Reg, who acts as guide throughout the preparation stages. You will get to know him and his garden pea techniques very well. (All will be revealed!)

Reading this book will help you learn easy-to-master tools, skills and techniques for public speaking. Then, as you put them to use yourself, you will create and confidently deliver your own memorable wedding speech.

Read, enjoy and be successful.

Chapter One—Meeting and Falling in Love

This was probably the closest Connor had come to becoming a smoker again. He thought to himself, "Why on flipping earth did I agree to do this? I know he's my best buddy, but this is crazy." He was in the hotel car park again, dressed in his garden pea pod fancy-dress outfit. Breathless and pacing up and down, he was tucked away at the back of the waste bins, where nobody would see him. In a serious panic of a head-spin, he thought, "I can't do this. How can I get out of this nonsense? For goodness sake, someone help me!" As he walked about frenetically, he repeatedly looked down at a couple of small, scruffy pieces of paper in his right hand; then, up again to the sky. His high level of loyalty to his best friend was overridden by panic, confusion and a heart that was about to burst through his chest.

More thoughts, "That's it, I'll disappear. I'll leg it." While mumbling to himself, many thoughts clashed in his mixed-up head. "I know. I know. What a nightmare. Should have listened to that rubbish about those flipping garden peas."

"Where's Connor? He's gone again!" Ashley was getting more and more agitated.

Gerry was quite calm, "Look, son, he won't let you down. Stay focused. He must be somewhere here in the hotel."

"Yes, but this is the third or fourth time since the beginning of the ceremony that he's wandered off."

"And he's come back every time." Gerry was doing his best to reassure Ashley.

"Yeah. This time it's different. Nobody's seen him for a good half an hour."

"Stay calm. He's your best man. On one of the greatest days of your life. All will be fine."

"Best man? I'm feeling that I should never have asked him to do it. What on earth is his speech going to be like? That's if he comes back. If he's even written a speech."

Many people in that situation feel exactly like Connor. Research has revealed that most people would rather die than give a speech in public. They experience a pounding heart, sweating, panic, breathlessness and cannot shake the urge to be somewhere else rather than getting up and speaking in public—all because they had not fully prepared for their wedding speech. However, if you follow this true-to-life story with its real characters, and put its advice into practice, you will be totally successful.

Gerry did not need to reply to Ashley, as the best man suddenly reappeared. Ashley, visibly frustrated, demanded, "Connor, where on earth have you been? Nobody has seen you for at least thirty minutes. You keep going missing."

Connor pulled himself together and was back to his usual blasé self, "Keep your shirt on, Ashie bruv! Don't worry, I'm fine. Just needed to have a quick look at my speech notes."

Ashley was surprised, "Oh! You've actually made some, then! Thought you said you were going to wing it?"

"Look Ashie, my old matey. Have I ever let you down? How many times have I said, 'It'll be alright on the night?'"

"It'll be alright? You don't look as confident as you sound. You look rather sheepish to me; pale, very pale, green even! You're quivering like a leaf and, if you ask me, you look quite bizarre in that outfit."

As far as the rest of the group were concerned, Connor had not done anything towards his best man's speech. Connor tried to reassure the groom, saying, "Look matey, I said right from the beginning I am going to rely on those stories I tell down the pub about you, and snippets from anything that happens on the stag. Trust your old pal Connor. Okay, bruv?"

"Yes. I mean No! Look, I know what you said, but with your speech being the most anticipated, you might at least have done some proper preparation."

Confident Connor was actually nervous, "Proper preparation? Very clever! Well I was doing that in the car park, wasn't I, bruv?"

A resigned and now rather edgy Ashley said, "You're such a loser sometimes! Well, at least you're here now. Let's get on. We will be going in for the reception soon."

Although quite terrified, Connor now put on a brave and happy, smiling face, "So what do you think of the outfit, Ashie baby?"

Ashley looked him up and down, "You look ridiculous but funny at the same time. I'll give it to you, it's appropriate. So glad you didn't wear it during the ceremony, though."

"And hey! It'll look great in the pics. Don't you think?"

Ashley shook his head, "You just had to do something outrageous. Come on, let's mingle."

Most people who knew Connor were not surprised with his outfit. Those who did not know him or what it represented just stared in amusement and wonderment.

Ashley turned to Sophie, his bride, "It's okay. As you can see, he's back, and I can only guess that dressed like that he's going to do a bit of mickey-taking about the peas."

She whispered back, "We ought to continue mingling."

So, with the wedding ceremony over, the new Mr Ashley and Mrs Sophie Jamison got back to mingling with the family and friends outside the wedding breakfast room. They were soon to be seated next to each other at the circular top table with their parents. With a shaky smile, Ashley felt the need to quickly remind Connor of something. "Connor, remember you are not on the top table. You're on the next table, table two, with your parents and a few of our other close friends, so I will not be able to hold your hand anymore."

Behind that smile, Ashley's mind was in a bit of a spin. One moment, he was really pleased with himself, thinking about what he and Sophie had at last just achieved. Then, his mind was back in the reception area of the hotel where he and Connor arrived earlier that day. "The aim of getting here long before the wedding guests is so we can settle in. We need to get the feel of the whole place including where the ceremony and the reception are taking place, in the old barn. I need to run through my speech once again in the barn so my mind is clear when I welcome everybody as they arrive, later."

Connor? He just quickly shrugged his shoulders and grunted.

Sophie had stayed at the hotel the night before with her mum and the maid of honour, Sarah. Because of this, Ashley approached a member of the staff outside the dining room and asked, "Could you tell me if my bride, Sophie, in room 210, has had her breakfast? I'm not superstitious, but I'd better not see her till the ceremony."

The smartly-dressed young man said, "Not a problem sir. I'll check the list for you. Room 210 did you say?"

"Yes, Sophie Dale. There were probably three of them. She would've been with her mum and the maid of honour. Can you find out quickly? I don't want to bump into them."

Although Ashley was in a hurry to know the answer, the staff member walked off into the dining room very casually. Soon, he returned and said, "Yes sir, all three have finished and are gone. You're in the clear."

Ashley was relieved, "Thank you so much. Come on Connor, let's have our breakfast." Suddenly, his mind shot back to the present and to his speech. He turned to Connor and spoke quietly to him, "How do you feel now, matey? Are you sure you're going to be okay? You didn't sound too confident earlier."

Connor just smiled, and in a very firm manner said, "Ashie, matey, have I ever let you down? I'm not going to, today, either. And I don't need my hand held, thanks. On your bike..."

"Connor, it's just that I know that even following Reg's peas by preparing properly, I'm still panicking slightly over my speech. So, I'm concerned about how you are really feeling, having done so little."

Was this going to lead to a disaster through lack of preparation? He then thought to himself, "I know Reg's peas are going to come in handy and help me through this."

Suddenly, a member of the hotel staff called everyone to order, saying, "Ladies and gentlemen—your attention, please! The barn is ready. Please follow me." So, everyone turned and stepped forward towards the covered pathway which led to the barn behind the hotel, where the wedding breakfast was to be held. Both Ashley and Connor were sweating over their individual speech responsibilities.

How were the speeches going to proceed?

As everyone moved forward, Sophie's dad (Howard), walking slowly at the front of the moving crowd, stopped rather abruptly.

Sophie was right behind him. "Dad. Are you okay? What are you doing?"

Howard stood on the bottom step of the staircase leading up to a side room. He gained everyone's attention by gently tapping a glass with a spoon. "Oops. Sorry, darling. Don't worry. Trust me."

Everyone stopped in their tracks and were now facing him. Just over ninety sets of eyes looking at him. He repositioned himself a little further up the stairs, so his head was just a bit above everyone else's.

Sophie looked at her dad and spoke to Ashley, "Crikey! Look at his face. He's as white as a sheet."

"This isn't like your dad. He said he wasn't going to give a speech. What on earth is he doing?"

Howard looked and sounded worse than anxious Connor. Just as he started to speak, Connor, who had come to a sudden halt, shouted, "Oh, sugar!"

Sophie was right next to him, "Oh no, Connor's tripped over the bottom of his ridiculous outfit!"

Two of the five massive peas that had been attached with Velcro to the front of his outfit fell off and rolled to the bottom of the staircase.

Nobody was prepared for what was to come next.

Reg's Podcast

"Many people who need to give a speech at a wedding feel just like Connor. It's normal to have the jitters—perfectly natural to feel that way. The best way to overcome the jitters or anxiety is to be fully prepared. This means getting the speech written, with some practice of the delivery done way in advance of the event."

It had all started three years earlier...

A frustrated Ashley, feeling quite despondent, mumbled, "If we don't find anything soon, we're not going anywhere for our summer holiday this year."

Connor was also getting a bit cheesed off, "Yes, I know matey. We've looked at almost every hotel and resort in Barcelona, but nothing has grabbed either of us. I want a place by the sea with some activity."

Then, out of the blue, Ashley's eyes brightened, and he nudged his best mate, "Hey! Look at this one in the town of Cambrils, a bit down the coast from Barcelona."

Excitedly, Connor stood up with the laptop in his hands. "Hang on, clever clogs, hang on, let me read it."

"That's it, Connor. Positively perfect."

A few seconds passed while Connor finished reading the information, "Totally with you Ashley, my old pal. Sunshine holiday, here we come!" They had found a neat little hotel specialising in breaks for their age group.

He continued, "Look at all the fantastic facilities! That pool with the swim-up bar is just beyond belief, matey! The water sports are right on the beach. The gym is better than at your club. I bet the bike hire provides top-end equipment. Goodness, we will be in our element. Oh! Then there's the bar, beer and..." tongue-in-cheek, "beautiful scenery. Wizard."

September soon arrived, and both guys flew off to their greatly anticipated sunshine destination. They arrived at their hotel in the early afternoon, after one of those no-sleep, up-very-early, seven-o'clock-in-the-morning flights.

Having booked in and put their things away in their room, they settled down in the swim-up, outdoor bar. Ashley was so pleased he had scrolled down another search-results page on his laptop and found this hotel. "So, here we are, two late-twenties, quite good-looking, fit guys on a holiday in a fantastic place, ready to lap up the sunshine. Hopefully, we'll meet some people to have some fun with. What frolics are we going to get up to?"

Connor lounged back in the armchair with his arms above his head, "Well bruv, for the rest of the day let's just wander around and see what's what in the town."

"Spot on, Connor. Finish your drink and let's get to it."

While in the bar, they chatted with some other holidaymakers. The conversation led them to wander through the picture-postcard town. Later in the evening, everything transformed. The place turned into a magnet for young people like them. The bars and clubs were booming. They had a truly exciting evening, returning to the hotel in the early hours of the next morning. And this was only day one.

As they approached the hotel, they saw a coach parked outside and a new wave of holidaymakers arriving. They walked into the reception area and there, standing close to the reception desk, were two young women who appeared to have just booked in. Two young men, two young women. So, they started to chat. Looking at his watch, Confident Connor was the first to speak, "Good morning ladies, hope you had a fantastic flight." Both the women looked at him with smiles and one said, "Yes, it was great thanks." The four of them chatted for a short while until Ashley and Connor offered to take the new arrivals' cases to their room for them. His offer was quickly accepted and, once fulfilled, everyone went their separate ways, having said goodnight.

The guys had had a great, relaxing day wandering around town, lazing about. They had enjoyed a few plates of tapas and an exciting evening out. All was rounded off by meeting two young women of similar age to themselves.

The young women's names? Sophie and Sarah.

Next day. Well, you know what is coming next. Of course, they bumped into each other again at breakfast. The two guys with recently acquired local knowledge approached the girls. Ashley was the first to speak this time, "Good morning. Hope you slept well and are looking forward to the simmering, sun-soaked, first day of your holiday."

Both Sophie and Sarah smiled, and Sophie said, "Thanks for helping with our cases last night. Do you fancy joining us for breakfast?"

Ashley and Connor looked at each other then back to the girls. Connor was quick off the mark, ahead of Ashley, "Too right we would. Love to, darlings." And Ashley, "It was a pleasure. We'd be delighted to join you."

All four smiled at each other, and the guys sat down with them. A typical Spanish breakfast followed; eggs, bacon, sausage, baked beans, tomatoes, and a slice or two of toast.

Breakfast led to sitting around the pool together. Instant friends. In a nutshell, the rest of the holiday was spent together most of the time. The four of them teamed up with other holidaymakers and had a magical time enjoying the venue's fantastic facilities and everything else a sunshine holiday brings. The highlight, however, was enjoying each other's company.

Ashley and Sophie got on extremely well, mainly because of their backgrounds and a similar interest in fitness, especially cycling. Their experiences at university and professional ambitions were also on the conversation list. All four new friends hired bikes and enjoyed early morning rides out into the local countryside when it was cool and clear of cars. There were a few daytime rides to other towns and villages, as well.

On one occasion towards the end of the guys' stay, Ashley and Sophie went out cycling together just before lunchtime into the hilly countryside. Cycling alongside each other Sophie said, "That looks like a cosy little cafe for a light lunch."

Ashley did not need much convincing as it did look quite neat, "If it's good enough for you, it's good enough for me."

They sat close and next to each other, looking out across the landscape towards the sea, visible a few miles away. With a cheeky glass of wine each and a plate of tapas on the table, they smiled and chatted. At one point, they simultaneously reached forward to take something from the plate of tapas, and their hands touched. Well, a bit more than a touch; they held position for a few seconds. They both turned and looked straight at each other. Sophie was the first to speak, "Oops. Sorry." Followed immediately by Ashley's rather awkward, "No, it… it was my fault." Eye contact lasted a little longer than touch. Was this the beginning of "something" between new friends? Or nothing at all?

All holidays come to an end, as did this perfect one. Everyone realised that it was time to return to the real world of work back home and the usual routines. Ashley and Connor had almost completed their ten days so, on their last night, the four new friends had a cracking night out together. This finished extremely late, with Ashley and Sophie parting with a friendly kiss. Following that, Ashley said to her, "Look, we've got on so well let's exchange phone numbers. I'll call you next week once you are home and we can arrange to meet up?"

Sophie immediately agreed and replied by saying, "Great idea."

The next morning, there was a little sadness in the air—the four had enjoyed a really sound time together and now it was time to separate and for the guys to depart from Cambrils. Although Connor and Sarah had got on well, there was no arrangement to make contact like the other two. Besides, Sarah had a regular boyfriend at home. And Connor was nowhere near ready to partner up with anyone. The guys left the girls to their remaining few days at the resort. Oh! Then there was that parting kiss between Ashley and Sophie. Connor could hardly contain himself as he and Ashley got on the airport coach and said, "'Ere you, that kiss! That wasn't a goodbye kiss, was it! What was it bruv?"

Ashley just turned to his best friend, smiled a magnificent, cheesy smile and said, "Lovely, isn't she?"

A few days later, as promised, Ashley did call Sophie and they met up, even though their homes were quite a distance apart. A really remarkable rendezvous took place, and from then on they were hardly apart. Yes, love blossomed.

A year later, while out cycling together, they stopped and sat on a lakeside bench. While holding hands, they suddenly found themselves talking about their wishes for a future together and the possibility of having children. They both looked at each other, straight into each other's eyes, just as they had at that country cafe back in sunny Spain. Simultaneously and completely unplanned, both said, "Let's get married." This led to some fantastic giggly laughter, a massive, loving hug, and even more slushy, positively passionate smooching.

Sophie was the first to speak and said, "Wow! What have we just agreed?"

At that stage, neither of them were fully considering what getting married really entailed. All they thought about was each other, living together, getting hitched, and having love-made little monsters. Oh, and a little bit of cycling and fitness training thrown in. Those little monsters did not know what was in store for them. All the necessary arrangements leading up to that big, happy wedding day were furthest from their minds. All that was to come.

Chapter Two—What About the Speeches?

How many people meet like Ashley and Sophie? A magical meeting! Falling in love! Agreeing to marry! Fabulous!

After returning to their respective hometowns, Ashley and Sophie went on to spend a lot of time together, like most lovers and engaged couples do. A big chunk of those moments were in the gym and out cycling together, all loved-up. They met each other's families, and both of their circles of friends grew. And, of course, they carefully considered their plans for a future together. They were truly enjoying each other's company.

When asked about the wedding, Ashley would often say, "Well, that's still ages away." He was still not fully appreciating how much there was to organising a wedding, and how crucial it was to begin setting everything up as early as possible. This work became a regular topic of discussion with both sets of parents. Sophie's dad, Howard, although a rather hesitant chap, would occasionally ask "probing questions." So, rather than telling people what to do, he would ask, "Where are you going to live? What type of property is it going to be? Then there's the mortgage... Oh, and who's paying for the wedding?"

So, when a few such questions were fired at the happy, engaged couple, they generally did what was implied, or at the very least gave it some thought.

Both Ashley's and Sophie's families were quite traditional when it came to the wedding. This meant the women of both families getting themselves together to discuss many of the arrangements. Sophie, her mum Gwen, her best friend Sarah (who was to be her maid of honour) and Ashley's mum, Penny, regularly had a little gathering to discuss locations, flowers, dresses, hairstyles, and much more. That said, all final decisions were made by Sophie, who consulted Ashley in most things. She had made it very clear to Ashley, "There's one thing I will not discuss with you Ashley, my dress. Neither you nor anyone else except our mums and Sarah will see it until the wedding ceremony. Style, colour and length of the train are all being discussed behind closed doors. The only other exception will be Aunt Debra."

Since becoming good mates, Sophie's dad often travelled over and joined Ashley's dad, Gerry, at the local tennis and fitness club where Ashley did much of his indoor fitness training. Connor also got in there occasionally as a guest. This became a regular weekend thing when the men had their get-togethers. Not necessarily to talk about the wedding. It was usually sport, politics and television, with the wedding tagged at the end. All very manly business.

One Sunday lunchtime, all four men were chatting at the club and the wedding came up. "It's getting closer, boy," Gerry said to his son.

"What's that Dad? The end of the football season?"

"No, my boy. The wedding." Ashley was rather surprised with his dad's sharp response.

Ashley, however, replied casually, "It's all fine, Dad. Mum and the other women have got everything under control. They are doing a marvellous job with all the stuff they have decided to take care of. The venue has been booked for ages. Sophie and Mum are often asking for my views on things like the flowers and all sorts of other stuff. Hey, as you know, our suits are all ordered from the outfitter and will be ready for collection a couple of days before the big day. I think I will buy mine and keep it for the future."

"And what about a honeymoon?" Gerry added. "And then there's the best man and the ushers. You do have some responsibilities, you know." It was Gerry's turn to do what Howard regularly did.

Ashley sensed that, by the way Gerry was speaking, he was working his way up to something else. So, he asked him outright, "Come on Dad, what are you working up to?"

"Well, my boy," Gerry started, "there is one major responsibility that we have not touched on—the speeches. Traditionally, the people who usually speak at the ceremony and the reception are the bride's dad, you and the best man. We are all here right now."

"Yes, I know all that, Dad, and maybe we should be doing something." Hesitant Howard heard something about speeches and remained strangely quiet, suddenly immersed in deep thought. Had the subject of speeches touched a nerve? Was Ashley avoiding this important aspect of this major event in his life? And, why was Howard so noticeably quiet?

Connor joined in and said, "Come on guys. Twaddle talk. It's ages away. That sort of nonsense can be done the week before. Gassing about the stag do is far more interesting. Come on Ashie baby, where do you fancy?" The men suddenly agreed and started discussing where the stag should take place instead of talking about the speeches. All in denial?

Ashley spoke directly to Connor, "Whatever we do or wherever we go, you are arranging it. As best man, you are responsible for that."

Connor, in his usual style, simply shrugged his shoulders, "Task accepted, matey. I want to hear what others have to say before offering my suggestion, though. Ash, where and what do you fancy?"

"Well, the options are so vast! Places like Prague and Berlin are quite popular. We would need to research them properly and find out what activities are available, wherever we end up choosing to go."

Gerry was thinking so hard that his face seemed to changed shape. Very seriously, he said, "I was thinking of somewhere much closer to home. Somewhere on the coast so we can go sea fishing."

Howard was standing back as usual, and needed a prompt from Connor, "Come on Mr H. Your contribution?"

"I'm really out of touch with this sort of thing. I'll go along with anything you all agree with."

As Connor had raised the subject, everyone was now looking at him. Looking straight back at them he said firmly, "It's obvious. It can only be one place, and that's Barcelona. It's where Ash and I wanted to go before bumping into Sophie and Sarah in Cambrils." Amazingly, they all stood with eyes wide open, smiling in agreement.

With a massive smirk on his face, Ashley said, "What a fantastic idea. Job done! Barcelona it is. Blow me, that was easy! Thanks, Connor. See? He is good for something, Dad."

Gerry commented on the agreement, "Fine by me, and a good reason for going there. Nice and warm. And it's on the coast, so we could still go sea fishing."

It ought to be noted here that Howard still remained rather quiet and a little thoughtful. This was evident in his eyes, as he closed them slightly. Yes, he was deep in thought. The rest of the men carried on enjoying their chat and, having agreed on the location, Ashley needed to give Connor a reminder. "Now Connor, remember, you are responsible for arranging everything to do with the stag. Let's take it that one activity, while we're away, is going sea fishing."

"No problem, boss. We can draw up a list of those being invited, and I'll find us somewhere inexpensive and as close to the beachfront or the port as possible. Job jobbed."

Ashley had to have the last word, "And do it as soon as possible. You know what trouble we had finding a place last time."

A bit later, as they were all walking through the car park to be collected, Howard sidled up to Ashley as he was getting close to his lift home and said, "Your dad has a point. So, what are you doing about the speeches?"

"Yes, I know. It's just that the wedding seems so far away. I've been telling Connor that he ought to get the stag arranged as soon as. So, I suppose I should do the same with my speech. I'll give it some thought."

"Also, think about how nice it would be for you and Connor, the traditionally-appointed speakers, to get your heads together. You could link your words to make it really interesting for the guests. Just a thought."

Ashley liked Howard. He did not give an answer, though. He just shrugged his shoulders and made a moaning sound as if he wanted to avoid the topic. As he got into Sophie's car, he thought to himself, "He only said, 'You and

Connor." He didn't mention himself. As father of the bride, isn't he one of those expected to speak, as well?" By that time, it was too late to follow up on this. They had all said cheerio, and were off to their respective homes.

A few days later, Ashley was at Sophie's home for an evening meal with her and her parents when the subject of the wedding came up in conversation. Nothing much, just chit-chat. It came up again between Howard and Ashley when they were in the kitchen, doing the washing-up. In his usual, casual, quiet manner Howard said, "Have you thought any more about the speeches, Ashley?"

Ashley looked from side to side, thoughtfully, and said, "Well, I had a chat with Connor during the week, and he's still thinking about putting something together after the stag event, so he's got more to talk about. You know what he's like. He leaves most things till the last minute, and he's still usually successful in whatever he does."

"That's Connor. What... what about you?"

"Well, the last time I gave a presentation to any sort of audience was at university and it wasn't too great an experience. There was no instruction. Everyone was bored rigid, even though we were expected time and again to give these presentations to the rest of the group. Being honest, I haven't got a clue how to go about it. I suppose that's why I've been avoiding it."

"Look, Ashley, Gwen has been talking with a guy she knows at the gardening club." Gwen was quite a keen gardener and grew a small amount of fruit and vegetables at home for their family.

Just then, Gwen walked in, having heard part of the conversation, and said, "Reg used to be a Toastmaster and officiated at loads of big functions, including weddings. He has also worked with people to create speeches and presentations of all sorts. I could have a word with him to see if he'll help you. Maybe help more of us where necessary. I've had to give presentations at work over the years at various meetings, but never known how to do it properly. Like you, I don't really know what is expected, nowadays."

Ashley, at last, reluctantly showed signs of interest. "Alright, you've pinned me against the wall. This Reg guy. How do I contact him?"

With a little support from his wife, Howard had achieved his goal. A little seed had been planted, some water poured on, and it had finally germinated. Just like gardening.

Both Howard and Gwen were so pleased with themselves. Gwen said, "Leave it to me. I'll arrange something and let you know how to contact him."

As they finished wiping up, ready to sit and chat more about the main topic of the day, Howard added, "As strange as it may seem, he's a bit of a dab hand with peas throughout the whole year."

Ashley said, "Peas? What on earth do you mean 'peas throughout the year'? Can't wait to meet this gardening, public speaking and pea expert, Reg."

Reg's Podcast

"It's interesting how many people regard speeches as something minor, when it comes to weddings. While leaving it till the last minute may be okay for some, it is not the best course of action for the majority of people—especially those who are not used to creating and delivering presentations. I recommend that, as soon as a couple get engaged, initial speech plans should be drawn up. Nothing elaborate, just minor notes and a bit of research about what is expected to be said. Early action prevents later panic and perspiration."

Chapter Three–Introduction to the First of Reg's Peas–Getting Started

"Really nice to meet you, Ashley. Gwen speaks very highly of you. I suppose she ought to, if you're to marry her daughter." Ashley was at Reg's home, walking with him to the kitchen.

As they walked they chatted, "Yes, she's a really nice lady and Howard's a nice guy. Level-headed, quiet people. They've told me that you're a bit of a wizard when it comes to speeches of all sorts. Especially wedding speeches." There was a very slight pause, "Oh! And a bit of a dab hand with peas, apparently."

"Wizard? I suppose that's a matter of opinion, but I do have quite a bit of experience behind me when it comes to these sorts of things, especially wedding speeches. So, you've heard about my peas, then."

Ashley responded, "I'm interested to hear how you grow peas all the year round."

Gentleman Reg now had a broad glowing smile on his face, "Ah! That means you know something about my peas—but not everything I guess. All about them will be revealed soon enough." Reg turned on the kettle and asked, "Tea?"

Mr health and fitness, Ashley, nodded and said, "Yes please. Green if you've got it."

"No problem. I take the same." The efficient side of Reg did not waste any time getting the conversation on target, "When did you last give any form of presentation to a group of people in a formal setting?"

"The last time I gave a presentation, of any description, was back at university and I'm now occasionally asked to speak at meetings at work. That's it. I must admit this wedding speech business is a bit daunting for me. Especially with everything else that's happening with the event. I've never had any formal training or coaching. Never been on a proper presentation skills course."

"Yes, getting married makes for some very exciting times. I remember my wedding very vividly." They stayed in the kitchen while Reg made the tea. Reg continued talking, "Interestingly, my father-in-law helped me with my speech. It was very simple and basic. I just got up, thanked a few people, handed out a few presents and sat down. Probably, the most memorable thing about it was that I had to get back up again when my best man, John, reminded me that I hadn't mentioned the surprise gift intended for my new wife. I was so nervous that everyone in the room was a complete blur to me. Could hardly see them! John tugged on my jacket sleeve and handed me the little box. I then announced the significance of it to everyone. Wow! You should have seen and heard the response—everyone clapped like mad and thought I'd forgotten the present on purpose for effect. Not so, but they didn't know that. My wife and I often talk about it. That small bit was so effective that people are still talking about it, all these years later. Really memorable."

"Well Reg, on that basis and with your experience since then, do you think you could help me with mine?"

"No problem at all. If you follow everything we discuss and put it into action, you will end up giving such a speech that everyone will still be talking about it at your silver wedding anniversary. We can create something they'll all recall, just like the guests are still mentioning my unintentional blunder. We can make yours better and more memorable. That last word is important—remember it, memorable."

They picked up their mugs of green tea and walked out into the garden.

At the bottom end of the garden was Reg's shed. Ashley stopped in his tracks, "Shed? That's more like a bungalow. It's spread right across the full width of your garden." There were two doors, one at each end of the front, facing the garden. The wooden door on the left was swinging in the light breeze. As they got closer, Ashley noticed a plaque on the outside, just above the door. The words Reg the Veg and a couple of pea pods with some loose peas around them were delicately engraved on it. "Quite appropriate for a garden shed," he thought to himself. Inside, there were four old armchairs, two of them pulled close together.

"Here we are Ashley, let's sit on the best two. As you can see, down there is my gardening stuff, and I do my other work down here, in the summer house section."

Ashley looked around and took in the difference between the two ends. He noticed a few pictures on the walls of the summer house end. Nearly all of them, in some way or another, featured garden peas.

Reg brought Ashley's attention back to him, and they chatted about all sorts of things while drinking their tea. Then Reg said, "So let me tell you how I got into this public speaking lark."

He continued, "Well, I had been a management trainer during my first career and, on retiring early, I became a teacher in adult education at a couple of colleges for a short while and branched out as a self-employed management trainer. Then, after that, I trained teachers on how to teach and trainers on how to train."

"So, how did you move into this public speaking business?"

"Well many of the skills that teachers and trainers use to deliver a message are the same as those needed in delivering a speech. Someone invited me to run some presentation skills courses applying those skills. Things have grown since then, and now I help people with job interview presentations, social event talks and business presentations."

"Gwen said you've worked as a Toastmaster as well."

"That's right. I officiated at all sorts of events, including weddings. That interested me so much that I started specialising in helping people with wedding speeches."

Ashley was quite impressed with what he had heard, and rounded it off by saying, "Wow! Impressive!" Then, he asked, "So, what happens now? How do we do this?"

"Well, it's quite straightforward, really. I'll help you create a speech and then share with you the techniques to deliver the speech. I find that the difficulty for most people, apart from getting started, is finding the confidence to actually get up in front of others and speak. If you believe the research, most people would rather die than give a presentation to a group of people. The truth is that it's no different from having a chat with people in a club or in a bar. In fact, anywhere, just like us right now. The difference is that there are usually more people and it tends to be a bit more formal."

"Mmmmm. Interesting. Never really thought about it that way. Well, I've never had to. You're already beginning to get me thinking differently."

"No, most people don't see it that way. The skills needed are exactly the same as you and I are using right now. We use them on an unconscious level."

Ashley was a little puzzled, "Unconscious?"

"Yes, we communicate most of the time without even thinking about it. In addition to sharing the techniques, I'll coach you so you can employ those skills properly and on a conscious level. You will be able to query anything we discuss and contact me anytime for advice and guidance. Does that suit you?"

"Sounds good to me. What happens next?

"Well, if you're happy for us to work together...."

"Which I am."

"Okay. I usually find that most people I work with need just a few hours together. However, you'll also need a bit more time to do the planning and preparation at home. And that's where we start. You must have heard this before, 'Failing to plan is planning to fail.'"

"Yes, I've heard it many, many times—Dad mentioned it the other day when the topic of the speeches came up. That's why I'm here. I've a feeling that my best man may be failing to plan and will leave it till the last minute. I want my speech to be a knockout. I want to be successful."

"And you will be, as long as you put a little effort into it. So, if you're ready, let's get straight into it."

Reg explained the process that he had adopted to help people with all sorts of presentations, speeches and training sessions. Ashley agreed to this, "So, I will get back to you within a week with a list of my first thoughts on content for my groom's speech. It'll follow a traditional format of introducing the guests to my wife, thanking people for attending, then thanking those who have made the event possible and giving them gifts."

"That's it. Just a list at this stage. Take it easy. Put all the information into a Word document or in a notepad which you dedicate to the speech and nothing else."

"That's a good idea. I've got a decent tablet so will probably put my notes there first and use a memory stick as a backup."

Reg nodded his head in agreement, "That's great. The last thing you want is to do all the work only to lose the information. Keep a copy of everything and keep it all safe."

Ashley started thinking ahead and said, "So, beyond the traditional format stuff, I suppose I need to think about how to make the speech more personal for everyone. Maybe think about little stories that the audience would find interesting, especially stories about Sophie and myself."

"Ashley, you are ahead of the game here. Stories are especially important—we will come back to this as time goes on. Think how comedians use stories to bring their humour alive."

Ashley was nodding all the time as Reg was speaking, "Up to this point, Sophie and I have known each other for coming up to two years, and we've had many adventures. It would be great to share some of these with family and friends, especially the light-hearted ones."

Reg re-emphasised, "Just like comedians, remember to keep it simple. Just notes at this stage. Make sure you record the ideas as you think of them. This frees the brain to think about something else rather than having the same thought running around in your head over and over."

"Thanks, Reg. Having heard several disastrous wedding speeches over the years, I'm determined to make this speech something to be remembered for all the right reasons, unlike some of those others."

Reg was not quite ready to stop yet, "Ashley, as you create the list, consider the purpose of your speech. Every presentation, no matter what it is for, whether social, business or any other reason—including your wedding—must have a purpose."

"A purpose? Meaning what?"

"There's got to be an intention, an objective for the speech. So, consider what you're trying to achieve."

Ashley was at a bit of a loss and started scratching his head, "I don't want to come across as a bit thick here, but this isn't making sense."

"Okay. Everything we do ought to have a purpose. In our situation, with your speech, knowing what that purpose is means you know what you want to achieve. This will help you create the list and ultimately turn that into a script."

Ashley added, "Well, grooms have to give speeches. You're going to tell me it's more than that aren't you?"

Reg simply said, "Yes."

"Hang on. I'm getting it. There was an expression we heard a lot at uni, 'Start with the end in mind.' This gets us to think about where we are going and why we are going there."

"You're on the right track now, Ashley."

"So, my purpose or intention is to share some information and things of interest, while also entertaining our guests."

"You've got it. The purpose of a wedding speech is to thank, inform, interest and entertain. Keep that in mind all the time, from now on."

"Phew. That had me really lost for a while, but I've got it. Those years at uni weren't wasted, were they!"

Purpose

Once you have accepted an offer to speak at a wedding, it is wise to establish the exact objective and desired outcome of the speech. Whatever role you have at the event, there are traditional outcomes. It is best, therefore, to do some research to find out what those demands are. Make sure you talk with the person who has invited you to speak. They will give you an idea of what they want. The purpose is usually to thank individuals for being present at the event and for the wedding gifts, to share some information and to entertain. Depending on the role of the speaker, it is often expected to be sharing a story or two about the bride and/or groom.

Ask yourself: What is the Purpose? Am I achieving the Purpose? Did I meet the Purpose?

"Look, Ashley, I don't want to overburden or confuse you with too much information today. Let's cut it there."

"Must say Reg, it's been a great first session. This is fascinating."

As they both got up out of the armchairs and were leaving the shed, Ashley referred to the engraving above the door. "Hey Reg, I like the engraving up there."

"I'm glad you noticed it. You'll get used to the peas as we work together." Ashley was puzzled by this so asked what Reg meant by it. "Well, it's like this. In a nutshell, I was on a presentation skills course many years back when introduced to what the trainer called the five Ps of presentation skills—**P**lanning, **P**reparation, **P**ersonality, **P**ace and **P**ause. Over the years, I've accumulated many more words that begin with the letter **P**, all of which are linked to the skills and techniques of public speaking. I've accumulated quite a bank of them and will tell you more about some of them as we progress with your speech."

"Wow! I think I get the drift. I guess that rather than having loads of facts about the skills each of the words beginning with P acts as a reminder of each of those skills and techniques that you refer to."

"You're spot on, Ashley. I think we're going to get on really well. Enjoy recording those thoughts about your speech. Oh, and think about the next of the Ps. We're at the planning stage, at this moment. Preparation continues right up to the moment you stand there to give the speech."

They shook hands and Ashley made a commitment, "I'll get some information back to you by the end of this week. That gives me six days."

"That's good by me, Ashley."

As Ashley walked away back through the garden and out via the side gate, his head was beginning to buzz with ideas.

He was also thinking of something Reg had said during their conversation "Make your wedding day speech so memorable that everyone who witnesses it will still be talking about it at your silver wedding anniversary."

Reg's Podcast

"It's best to start considering the purpose of the speech: to thank, inform, interest, and entertain the guests. So get on with the note-taking at this planning and preparation stage as soon as the engagement is announced. Follow the traditional content of a groom's speech, creating a simple list which can be enlarged later.

Yes, many people get a bit het up over the skills used in a speech, but the truth is that they're the same as those used in any normal conversation. Though we generally use them automatically and unconsciously.

I will repeat this many times—just remember— Failing to Plan is Planning to Fail."

Chapter Four—Beginning to Put It Together

"What do you think, Connor?" Ashley had invited Connor to his home to discuss his meeting with Reg. "Howard made the suggestion. We could both go to Reg for guidance. We could learn a lot from him using his peas, then write our speeches independent of each other."

Connor, being Connor, was not convinced that starting to put a speech together so early in the proceedings made any difference. "What? You have got to be bonkers, matey. One—the wedding is ages away. And two—well, what on Earth have peas got to do with speeches?"

Ashley was not surprised by Connor's response. "Look, I want this wedding to be special. I only intend doing this once. People expect us to deliver speeches and mine is going to be as good as I'm able to produce. With a bit of help, it could be even better."

Connor was still not convinced, "And you reckon this old Reg geezer and his peas will do it for you?"

Ashley replied, his frustration betraying itself, "He's a really nice bloke with loads of experience, and he's already started using his peas with me—we have started with the pea for the purpose of the speech and will move on to planning and preparation. It's dead easy to follow."

Connor was puzzled and sarcastically said, "Peas! Oh, how purposeful! How perfectly productive!" He drew a deep breath, "Peas? I'm mystified. And just don't get it. But then, to shut you up I'll think about it. It might be interesting just meeting this guy. Anyway, all there is to this public speaking malarkey is get up and speak, then sit down quickly. Job jobbed."

Ashley responded, "Even I know there's more to it than just getting up and speaking. I've spent the last few days making a list. Look, if you're interested and free, maybe I can contact Reg and ask if you can join us at the next meeting."

Connor huffed, puffed, and drew a deep breath. "That's it, then. I tell you what I'll do. Compromise. Next time you go and see Mr Peas in this shed place of his, yeah, take me with you. Don't expect me to change my mind on this, though, matey." He shook his head, huffed again and added, "Peas!"

Ashley was surprised beyond belief with this. "Well, that's a bit of a quick turnaround. You're on. We can go together. In the meantime, I've agreed to send him an email with my first thoughts so he can offer some more advice. I'm saving them on my tablet and a memory stick."

"Peas, planning, memory sticks. Twaddle. But, yeah, I'll go with you. Don't think I'm going to start a list or do anything else, though."

Planning

Armed with the purpose, it will be time to sit down and start making some initial notes about what you intend to say. This can be made simple by making them on a notepad or a dedicated file on a computer. Think about what you must, should, and could speak about. This will include what you believe the audience will want to see and hear.

Ask yourself: Who shall I obtain information from? What must, should and could be covered?

Ashley needed to share with Connor what he had achieved so far. "Okay, true to the agreement with Reg, I've already started on the pea for planning. So far I've concentrated on the guests who are invited, those who need to be thanked, and I plan to find a few things that Sophie and I have experienced since being together. After all, I need to focus on her."

Still feeling the need to be negative Connor said, "Oh how wonderfully pppperfect."

"Just you wait. You'll meet someone. Love will catch up with you one day, and you won't be so glib, then." Ashley was getting a little fed up with Connor's attitude, but then he had been putting up with it for years, since school.

Because of Connor's manner, Ashley decided not to tell him any more about the new file on his tablet, Ashley's Wedding Speech. As soon as he had a fresh thought, he quickly wrote it on a notepad or his smartphone so that he could think of other ideas. His plan was to build upon the words later: extending them into sentences on his computer or tablet. He realised that losing this valuable material would be disastrous. The stick was a form of backup and allowed him to work when away from his own devices.

During the following week, Ashley discussed suitable material with all sorts of people in the two families. One evening, he managed to have a quiet word with his future mother-in-law. "Gwen. Thanks for putting me in touch with Reg. He's already got me working on my speech. I've managed to get the traditional basics and now need to add some suitable stories. Stories about Sophie and I."

Gwen had ideas of her own so was more than willing to help out, "Yes, Reg is a nice guy. As you know, Howard and I've been talking lots about the wedding in general and, just lately, the speeches."

"Thanks, Gwen. I'm looking to find something from Sophie's past that can be added. Something that is personal to her. Maybe something dating right back to when she was much younger, before she and I met. It needs to be a topic that people will find interesting. Reg wants me to find something that'll intrigue our guests so much that they will still be talking about it at our silver wedding anniversary."

"It sounds like you need a little story that will get everyone emotional. Weddings are emotional to start with. A story will make it even more so."

Ashley agreed, "Yes, that's right. It's the sort of thing that Howard will need for his speech as well."

"Howard? Hasn't he told you? He's decided…"

Gwen was not able to finish what she was about to say because Sophie suddenly appeared. They had not heard her coming. "What are you two cosying up about? The way you both look, it must be something I'm not supposed to hear."

Ashley had trouble hiding his obvious embarrassment, but managed, hesitantly, to get some words out, "Well, errr, to be honest, it was and… it's a secret. And you won't be able to twist my arm."

She was a little taken aback. Jokingly, she mimicked him. "Well… err… to be honest—I hope it was a secret—like—about the most expensive, extra special, super-duper, mouth-watering present you can't afford. And you're going to give it to me in front of all our guests at the wedding. And I'm going to love you even more for it."

Laughing, Ashley and Sophie fell into a hug and a smacker of a kiss. Ashley mused, "What a good idea. Give her something super-duper in front of everyone. But what, and how? Reg did say—something special. Maybe do or say something special."

They all laughed so loudly about this that Howard put his head around the door, "Can anyone join in?"

Gwen winked at Ashley and, when Sophie was not listening, whispered, "I'll have a word with Howard about it. We'll find that something special to get them all emotional. That said, I might already have just the thing for you. Something that means so much to her."

Ashley was pleased with himself. Within the short period of time agreed with Reg he had scratched out a very rough list. He was careful to keep this all away from Sophie; everything was to be a surprise on the day of the wedding.

Here is what he put in his first effort—

- A welcome to everyone present—on behalf of "my wife and I".
- A mention of those who had travelled long distances.
- Making a comparison with something else that happened in history on the date of the wedding.
- Comment on how I feel—dreading giving the speech and hearing what the best man might be saying (especially about what happened on the stag event).
- Comment about weddings being about love and happiness, and looking forward to the future with Sophie.
- Toast to absent friends and family.
- A few thanks on behalf of both my wife and myself—mentioning individuals by name.
- Reference to lack of the traditional wedding favours on the tables—wanting to use a portion of the wedding fund to donate to a cancer research charity and the reason for it.

- Thanks directed to all the parents for their help and guidance during the planning of the day.
- Thanks to in-laws for bringing up such a lovely daughter and for welcoming me into their family.
- Further thanks to Mum and Dad for all their support and words of wisdom over the years, making reference to specific times when I tested their patience.
- Then—with my wife—gifts to be given to parents.
- Thanks to the bridesmaids and ushers—making a reference to the gifts given to them.
- Thanks to others for the music at the ceremony.
- A massive thanks to my wife for agreeing to marry me and a comment about how wonderful she looks.
- Reference to lessons learned since meeting Sophie.
- Toast to my wife.
- That something special for Sophie—whatever it is! (Don't know how it will be presented, yet.)
- Handover and introduction to my best man (unless we have an MC).

When sending the draft list as an email attachment to Reg, he acknowledged that there was much more to include. He was having difficulty finding something that would make the speech individual and memorable for everyone hearing it. He believed Reg would help him realise what it could be. And, of course, he had now enlisted the help of Sophie's parents and others.

On receiving and reading the information, Reg decided to telephone Ashley rather than reply by email. "Well done Ashley. Thanks for getting your work to me so swiftly. Many people leave this planning so late that they get very stressed by the last-minute rush to create a speech. You are well on top of everything."

"Thanks, Reg. As I said to you the other day, I feel my best man may be one of those who will get stressed by leaving it late. I'll bring him with me to our meeting this week if that's alright with you?"

"Good. I'll see what I can do to change his approach. Anyway, what you have achieved is very good and puts you on track towards a cracking draft script for the final speech. You've got the basic elements. Now identify some incidents involving you and Sophie since you first met, and any additional stories to make the speech more personalised, informative and memorable for everyone at the wedding."

Reg's reassurance was encouraging, "Thanks, Reg. I've already spoken with my future in-laws. Gwen says she has an idea. I'll get back to you soon on that."

"When you do, we can move on to turning the list into a first draft of the speech, but just stick to the list first."

Reg was sticking to the early pea of his pea pod process, establishing a list before rushing into a fully scripted version.

It was only a day before Ashley was back on the telephone as he had now added the following to his bullet points:

- Prepare to thank whoever speaks first—dad-in-law. Commenting on anything said of note. (Scout motto: 'Be Prepared')
- Mentioning by name close family members who are present.
- Plans for the honeymoon.
- Possible stories:

1. Details of how we met.
2. The wedding proposal.
3. Special story about something from Sophie's past.
4. The clashing of hands when first met.
5. There will be more to choose from.

- Gift to best man as a sweetener ahead of his speech.
- A memorable way of giving **something special** to Sophie.

Ashley was even more pleased with himself. "It hasn't been easy, Reg. There are so many things that I could mention, but I guess time will be tight on the day."

Reg was equally pleased, "Nice work, Ashley. Yes, you're right about timing. For your groom's speech, ten or so minutes is about right, twenty minutes maximum. Your guests won't want to sit there all afternoon listening to speeches. Okay. Let's move onto the next bit. You can now start putting some meat on the bones of your list and those stories Ashley."

Ashley was reluctant to share more information, "At this stage Reg, I don't want to share everything. The bit about Sophie's past needs a bit of secretive work by her parents so I want to keep it to myself for the time being. That said, I'll share some of the plan when we next meet."

"Fine. I won't push you on that. Look, as you've done so well, I think we'll postpone our arranged meeting as we can approach your speech a little differently from here."

Ashley was a little disappointed, "That's a shame. Connor was all fired up to meet you and quiz you about your peas."

"Please apologise to him for me. However, this early foundation work is so important, and you are on a roll, let's keep it going. We can afford to delay our meeting for another week. In the meantime, start pulling all those words together and create a draft of the speech. This will be the first version of your script."

Ashley felt things were heating up, "Blow me. How do I do that?"

Reg added some more reassurance, "It's fine. Once you've put this draft together, I'll help you with more information about structure. For the time being, go back to your first list and follow that pattern, point by point, to create this first draft. Slot in those other items from the second list where you think they are most appropriate."

"You're leaving it to me, then."

"At this stage, yes. It's so that you get to know your own material right from the beginning. This means that you have total ownership. By the time you deliver it at the wedding, you'll know it so well that you'll do it confidently and sound completely natural."

"Any tips?"

"Yes. Take each item on your list. Imagine that you're sitting at home talking with close friends about each of them. This will help expand your notes. Just remember to record them as soon as you can before the ideas go out of your head."

"Okay. Got that. You're the boss."

"Trust me. I promise you, everything will be brilliant. I'll guide you stage by stage. If you've any queries, just call."

The meeting was rearranged, and Ashley started thinking about how he was going to form the short notes into a more meaningful script.

Reg had let Ashley know that the next stage would be something to do with structuring the talk into three clearly defined segments and referred to it as another pea—

Parthenon. As Ashley put the phone down, he thought to himself, "Parthenon? I get the peas now, but how does the Parthenon connect with wedding speeches?"

Reg's Podcast

"To build a solid foundation for your speech create a list of the traditional topics and add anything special that you feel ought to be included. Search for something else that will cause the listeners to become interested and possibly a little emotional. Keep everything safe in a book or computer—have backups and copies as losing anything could be disastrous.

Once the list is complete, consider creating a first draft."

Chapter Five—Structure the Speech

Connor had been as disappointed as Ashley to have the meeting with Reg postponed, but here they were arriving at Reg's home on the rescheduled day. Even though Connor was a bit sceptical, he was still looking forward to the meeting. He could not get his head around the notion of peas being associated with wedding speeches, "Ashie, I'm quite looking forward to this! Too right I am. Peas. I just don't get it."

Reg's wife met them at the front door, "Nice to meet you both. Reg is in his shed getting things ready for you. He'd forgotten to put the peas up on the wall for you." She left them at the back door. "There you are. You can see him fiddling about down there with the armchairs."

As they walked, Connor smirked and said, "Hey. This gets more bizarre all the time. Putting the peas up on the wall! What the heck is going on?"

Reg shook hands with the two guys and was the first to speak, "Good to see you again, Ashley, and welcome to my shed... Connor, isn't it?"

As Connor was scanning the shed he made eye contact, "Thanks, Reg. Neat meeting you." Like Ashley had, he noticed the contrast between the two ends of the building. A posh end, and a not so posh end.

"Thanks, Reg. Good to be back. Looking forward to hearing what you thought about my first draft."

Reg was quite complimentary, "You did very well. I've just sent an email with some suggestions to help make it even better. It would be best that you read it when you get back home. Bear in mind my observations and suggestions are just that—you do not have to follow any of them. The choice is yours. Once you've read and digested them, we can speak on the phone."

"That's magic. Thanks, Reg."

"You'll find that as well as other stuff, what we talk about today is in my email. The next pea is important. It will help with the next draft."

Both Ashley and Connor were eager to hear more about the peas and how Reg used them in his coaching. Connor was surprisingly quiet. He remained reservedly eager to receive some first-hand information.

On entering the shed, both newcomers to the world of Reg's peas noticed many laminated pictures, sketches and words displayed on the walls. Ashley had not noticed so many of them during the previous visit. "Reg, your wife said you were putting the peas up on the wall. I now know exactly what she meant."

Reg explained, "Yes, sorry for not meeting you at the door. I normally display the peas when working with my clients. I've put them up so I can explain how I use them to you both easily."

Things began to click for Connor, "This P stuff is becoming a bit clearer now that I've seen these. All the words begin with the letter P and, as Ashie has explained to me, the pictures all seem to relate to the peas of public speaking. There's a garden pea theme here."

Reg said, "I'm glad he's told you a little about them. That means I don't have to go over it again. As you've both shown such an interest, I'll explain how I use my peas to help people deliver confident and memorable presentations. You'll almost certainly use them in your wedding speeches and in any future presentations. It's all very simple."

Ashley replied, "True. I'm sure that whatever you say will be helpful with the wedding speeches. Hopefully useful at work as well."

Connor being Connor firmly said, "I don't know about that. This wedding is the only time I'm ever giving a speech and should I ever get married, I'll leave that job to other fools. However, I'm interested in getting the low-down on your pea stuff."

"So let's get on. Firstly, thanks to both of you for being here and sorry for the postponement."

Ashley said, "Fully understand that Reg. It's very kind of you to do this. It gave me time to do that first draft."

Connor said something similar and with some hesitation in his voice, "Although sort of interested, I'm not sure I need it. Ashie's wedding is just a one-off situation. I feel top-end sceptical about the use of the peas. With respect Reggie, it all sounds a bit gimmicky to me."

Reg was not in the slightest bit affected or offended by Connor's comment and replied by saying, "If I were sitting where you are, I'd probably be thinking exactly the same. All I ask is that you listen, ask questions, and take from it whatever you want. If you don't like what you hear, you're free to tell me so. It's just my take on the world of public speaking. A bit gimmicky? Not for me, although you're free to call it that."

Connor was a little embarrassed and wished he had not spoken with such hesitation or mentioned the word gimmicky. While they all sat down on the armchairs, he just nodded with raised eyebrows, sat and waited for Reg to speak further.

"Well, looking up on my wall. Here you can see some of the pictures of my harvested peas. Ashley and I have covered purpose then planning. Preparation, however, covers everything and keeps going right up to the wedding. That's why they are sitting apart from the others which are all jumbled up. Now, which do you think is the next to be used in my coaching process?"

Preparation

The notes made during planning will be brought alive by extending them into a full script. Gather together the chosen props and other materials. Remember the Scout Association's motto 'Be Prepared' so get everything ready; notes, aids, resources, materials, props, visuals, absolutely everything.

Speak with family and friends to find appropriate stories to share with the audience.

One important feature, if possible, is to visit the location where the speech is to take place. See and feel what it will be like on the day of the event.

The list of things to consider at the preparation stage is almost endless. Start putting everything gained into a logical order.

Preparation runs like a golden thread right through, from planning to the day of the speech. Ensure it includes the peas that follow.

Ask yourself: How might the guests respond to the props? Are the stories appropriate and inclusive for everyone who will be there?

There were dozens of pictures of peas; large peas, small peas, peas in pods, pods on their own and even pea plants at various stages of growth. Ashley glanced around, looking at so many pictures and words that he got confused and admitted it.

Recognising Ashley's confusion, Reg said, "Yes, at first sight, it can be a little daunting. I'll add that the order in which the peas are used does change depending on the individual, their experience in public speaking and their needs. For example, someone wanting to speak at an anniversary of any sort may have a different need from that of someone speaking at a job interview, golf club dinner or annual general meeting. Or, in your case, a wedding."

Connor showed some excitement, "Wow! You cover a wide spread of people and events then Reggie."

"I think you'd be surprised who's sat in these chairs before you, Connor. All with differing levels of experience and need."

There was a short lull while Reg gave the guys time to think a little more about the next pea.

Then, rather than press them, Reg said, "My son Len drew all the sketches. He's quite talented. A talented cartoonist I've recruited to support my work with my peas." He then got back on track. "Right, now here's a topic I'll speak more of later—pictures—you'll always remember these pictures. Store that word in your memory. It's an important one as I'll come back to it."

Both just nodded, not really knowing what Reg was talking about or hinting at.

Connor spotted the small banner statement running along the top of the wall just below the ceiling above the pictures. It read–'Failing to Plan is Planning to Fail.'

Reg said, "Now that one stays up all the time as it's key not only to planning and preparation but the whole process of creating and delivering any presentation. It's also highly relevant to gardening through the seasons here in my garden. I'll be coming back to it later."

Ashley chipped in, "Yes, you mentioned that last time, but I had not noticed the words up there."

Connor seemed a little less daunted and spoke out, "So, going back to your little question about what's next. Ashie's attempt at an overview of what you have already covered was sort of helpful. Yes, the first peas are over on the left; purpose, then planning and preparation. I seem to recall Ashie saying something about Parthenon being next."

Reg got up from his chair, removed the Parthenon picture from the pack and placed it to the right of planning and preparation. "Yes, I did mention it, and yes, it is next and very important too."

Ashley's eyes widened, "I've been thinking about it since you first referred to it the other week. I keep asking myself, what on earth has the Parthenon got to do with public speaking?"

Connor just shook his head and smirked, while thinking much the same as Ashley. He just had to say something, "Neat picture your son has sketched out, Reggie." A very tongue-in-cheek comment.

"Thanks. It's simple—the Parthenon is a former temple on the Athenian Acropolis in Greece. It's said to be the most important surviving building of Classical Greece. It's a long-standing structure. Structure being the key word here. Speeches and presentations need structure. You can't waffle on or leap from one idea to another. However, when you put your effort into constructing a wedding speech properly it should be really successful."

Connor, being Connor, had more to say. "It's memorable if nothing else. But I still don't see the connection. Parthenon, structure. Fine. I hope you are going to spill the beans and explain. Beans, get it? Beans—peas!"

Reg responded, "Thanks, Connor. Yes, I do. You lighten a subject that for some can be a bit stuffy. Look, all will become clear right now." He set out the old and well-used, successful structure of a presentation; the beginning, middle and end. He explained that a speaker needs to introduce the audience to what they are about to hear, then tell them about it and then round off by telling them what they have just been told. Reg continued, "A simple way to remember this is BBC."

Connor was quick with, "What? Do you mean BBC—as in brussels, broccoli and carrots? Seems to fit with the peas and with being in a garden we can have a basket full of vegetables. And loads more pictures." He chuckled, another smirk on his face and added, "Hey, and add my beans to that."

Both Reg and Ashley found Connor's reaction quite humorous. Reg continued, "Now I like that. I really do like that. Maybe, Connor, I'll get Len to draw three of the vegetables and put them up on the wall for future clients to enjoy. However, in this case, my BBC stands for beginning of the speech, body of the speech and conclusion of the speech."

Reg went on to explain why he used his BBC—beginning, body and conclusion. "I use this as it's the format used in television news broadcasts. There is always a very clear structure or Parthenon. The newsreader begins by briefly explaining what they are about to talk about—the news highlights—they then talk more fully about the news

of the day—the body. And finally—as they often say—they conclude by returning to one or two features of main importance. Sometimes, they might introduce something new, usually of general interest and often light-hearted."

There was a supportive contribution from Ashley, "Hey Reg! I like this BBC bit. I'll always remember that one. As soon as you set that out, I can immediately visualise the TV news. All the channels do the same thing, don't they? They all have the highlights at the beginning then go on to explain what's going on at home and abroad in the body and then, as you say, finish off at the conclusion with something interesting, or they repeat something they've just referred to. And they use pictures—stills and videos—to support what's said."

He continued. "I like what I've heard so far and now need to reshape my script into this BBC format. Because of that, I'd like to break now. If you're willing to meet again, Reg, I'm certainly up for it."

"You're on target Ashley. And Connor, I don't mind your scepticism. Just bear in mind that this is simply a vehicle to help people latch on to the basic concepts. So, if you both want to continue, are you happy to come back here?"

Ashley immediately replied, "As good as done. What about you Connor?"

"Mmmm. I'll give your proposal some thought. Did you like that one? Proposal… get it?"

Ashley and Reg groaned, shaking their heads.

Parthenon

Remember how impressive and strong a structure the Parthenon is. This is something that every speech needs to have in the form of BBC. No, not the British Broadcasting Corporation but the Beginning, Body, and Conclusion. Some say the most impactive elements are your beginning and conclusion. Say or do something at the beginning to gain the attention of the audience, then maintain that attention through the body and leave the audience with a message at the conclusion to cause them to remember the speech and you the speaker.

Ask yourself: Did I gain the attention of everyone at the beginning? How did I do it? What reaction was there? During the body of the talk, what did I do to ensure the guests were informed and entertained? What did I do and say to ensure everyone would remember this speech for years to come? What about the conclusion? Why would they remember that so well?

Arrangements were made and, just as the newcomers to the peas were about to walk out of the shed, Reg offered a

parting tip. "Connor, you might like to do what Ashley has done by starting to make some notes. I'll leave him to explain further. Whatever you do, do it now, not right up close to the wedding. You'll regret it if you do. And Ashley, just apply Parthenon to your new draft. Ensure the beginning captures the attention of your audience. Then move on to the main theme or themes of your speech in the body and conclude with something memorable. Something that relates to what you've been talking about and the occasion."

"Sure will, Reg. I'll get back to you as soon as it's done."

Ashley and Connor thanked Reg for his time and departed. As they made their way towards their cars, Connor said, "So bruv, what d'you really think about all this peas stuff?"

Ashley had already shown his hand while talking earlier, "For me, it's worth its weight in gold. I like the idea of the peas rather than just latching onto the letter P. What's more, it's the whole package. His nickname, Reg the Veg, the garden environment. All coupled with his extensive experience. And bear in mind, I've never been anywhere near a course about public speaking. All new to me, so it's good to have a system to hook the concepts onto. The pictures of the peas are helping. They help make it real."

Connor was not so positive, "You'll end up having nightmares with peas rolling all over you." Connor had one of his cheeky smirks all over his face. "On a serious note, though, I'm sorry to have used the word gimmicky earlier. It's just the way I feel about it. However, I'll maintain an open mind and consider what he has said."

"Was there anything that Reg said you could use?"

"Ashie. You're pushing me now. I'm still writing nothing. That BBC stuff does make me think about how to finish, sorry, *conclude* my speech. It will knock you and Sophie out. Just you wait."

They parted outside Reg's front door and went their separate ways.

On his arrival home, Ashley went straight to his tablet and found Reg's email referring to the first draft of the speech. He followed Reg's comments and reshaped the whole speech, paying particular attention to its structure (Parthenon).

The fresh draft was forwarded to Reg.

Reg phoned Ashley the following day and was quite complimentary. He also gave some extra guidance about structure. "Ashley, your BBC is sound. I suggest you go back to it again and consider this information. It's a slight extension of what I have already shared with you."

Ashley was interested to hear what was missing in his redraft, "So what was wrong with that version Reg?"

"There was nothing wrong with it. I just feel you could make it more interesting, more captivating for your listeners."

"So how do I take it to the next level?"

"With the beginning or introduction, try saying or doing something that will get the attention of your audience. Maintain this attention through the body with interesting content. This is where you tell your stories and can be humorous, where appropriate. At the conclusion stage, again create something that encapsulates what you have been talking about. Something memorable. Maybe leave the audience with something to think about.

Questions, quotes, humour, pictures, props and displays are just a few examples of what to use at the beginning and conclusion stages. Something to tempt or tickle the imagination. How's that Ashley?"

Props

At an early stage, consider the use of visual material to support whatever you are thinking about saying. This can include photographs or virtually anything else that enhances the spoken words. Whatever you choose needs to be in tune with the occasion and the audience. Most props are usually a surprise for the audience, so keep the planned showing of these items to yourself. Maybe you do the talking and someone else displays the items. Remember, a picture speaks a thousand words.

Ask yourself: What can be used? What is appropriate? How shall I incorporate the item? Did it work?

Ashley replied, "That's clearer Reg. I think your comments are pointed towards the beginning and conclusion which

could be smartened up a little. Do something or say something to get that attention and leave them with something memorable."

Reg closed this angle with, "You've identified what could be smartened up, so I will not harp on about it." He moved on by querying why the honeymoon did not get a mention. Ashley responded "I've had a rethink. Are our guests really going to be interested in that?"

Reg was a little surprised by the question, "Ashley. Remember the keyword that I use, memorable. You want this speech to be memorable, don't you?"

Ashley couldn't say anything except, "Yes."

"Well, your speech refers to that first meeting over in Spain. Add the romantic fact that you are going back to visit that very same place to relive some of the experiences and feelings that were ignited at that meeting".

Although Reg could not see it, Ashley's face showed disagreement, "Yes, well I'm not totally convinced that our guests would be interested in this news."

Reg added a bit more. "Emotions. Be passionate. You are talking to people and people like stories— especially happy ones. Your little story with a return to where it all started is just what your guests want to hear. Tell me, what else have you left out that I don't know about?"

"Well..."

"Come on, out with it."

Ashley was now a little bit embarrassed, but continued, "Well... we have got a few days before flying off to the same place in Cambrils and have been offered the use of my firm's property, somewhere romantic."

"Come on, tell me more."

"Our firm has a little flat for the use of employees when on business at our Paris office."

"Let me guess. You've secured its use and are going there for those days between the wedding and the honeymoon."

"Well, it's going to be vacant and, to make it even better, it will be free of charge. Sophie doesn't know about it. We are going there for that couple of days immediately after the wedding."

"Ashley, there you are. What a fantastic ending to the speech and you can make it especially memorable as well. Remember the C of BBC. How about this? At the end of your speech, you hand over to Connor, your best man..."

"Yes."

"Remember the story I told about my own wedding? For effect, at the end of your speech, do something similar to me, but do it deliberately. Sit down. Have a quick word with Connor and then stand back up. If Connor gets up, ask him to sit back down. Then tell everyone that you'd forgotten to mention something about the honeymoon. This alone will get some people going for the tissues. Then add the bit about Paris. You will have even the hardest person in your audience gasping with emotion."

"Do you really think so?"

"This is exactly what I've been emphasising. Make it so memorable that your guests will be talking about it for months, years, if not still referring to it at your silver wedding anniversary. That's how impactive these little bits can be."

"Reg. You're a big softie."

"Yes, that's what my wife's been saying for years".

"I suppose I'd better get on then and tinker some more with my script. Boy, this is going to be good."

Ashley was also wondering what the next pea might be.

Reg's Podcast

"By placing more emphasis on the early planning and preparation of a speech, the jitters so many people experience will be reduced, and you will prevent perspiration closer to the big event.

When you structure using Parthenon—with a beginning, body and conclusion—the speech will be more interesting and memorable for the guests.

To make it even more memorable, tell emotional stories with passion. They create pictures in the mind of the listeners.

The aim is to ensure the guests are still talking about the event, especially the speeches, at your silver wedding anniversary."

Chapter Six—Now for the Delivery

"Well Connor, are you coming to the next session with Reg?" Ashley and Connor were at the gym for a swift fitness session before work early one morning. They were in the warm-up and stretching area. There was quite a bit of noise, not only from the music being played but also from the cardio and weights machines.

They were both lying face down on the floor doing some push-ups. Connor was not as fit as Ashley so he was panting a little as he began speaking. "I think the old boy's a decent geezer and means well and I'm sure you bruv are getting... loads out of all this peas stuff. But I'm not into this theory nonsense and prefer to get on with it in my own way when I'm ready. Stuff me... I thought I was fit, what with my job an' all that. This is hard graft... besides anything else, and... I know I'm repeating myself a bit... it's far too early for me to be thinking about starting anything bruv."

"Yeah. You don't sound too fit either. That sounds like a no, then."

"Correct buddy boy. Yeah. I'll do it… in my own time. Closer to your big day… Yeah, probably that morning, in the toilet. Just to tease you, though… my speech conclusion is gonna be brill."

"Can't wait. I promise not to mention it to you again then. However, I'll keep on at you about your fitness. You ought to get in here more often."

They dropped the subject right there, and got on with their short session, showered, parted, and were off to work.

Ashley decided to phone Reg from his office at work. While waiting for him to answer, Ashley recalled a conversation with him about owning the words of the speech. Ashley had kicked it off with a question. "Reg, with all the experience you have, why don't you write the speeches for people like me? Surely, it makes it easier for them."

He had replied, "Well, it's my belief that the person making the speech, having created it right from the beginning, will know the content really well. The speech creator knows the words better than anybody else. My role is just guiding the writer towards that confident, memorable delivery. They own it totally and get greater satisfaction knowing that. I just help them get there."

Ashley's thoughts were interrupted by Reg answering the phone, "It's me, Ashley."

"Well, how are things going Ashley?"

Ashley was out with a quick answer, "Fabulous, thanks! I feel good about the effort I'm putting into this and sense that I'll feel really pleased on the day knowing that I wrote it. The amendments have been made to fit in with the pea for Parthenon and I'm ready to move on."

"That's really good news. Send it over to me so I can have another quick look and offer suggestions if needed. By the way, what about Connor? How is he?"

"It's him I've called about, really. He's chosen not to come to our next session. Reckons he's better off doing his own thing nearer the wedding day."

"So be it if that's what he's decided. I hope he doesn't go on to regret that decision. As you've done well so far, may I suggest you help him? You don't want him to fall flat on his face on your big day and spoil it for you."

Ashley was not quite sure about that. "Although he's my best mate and runs a very successful business, he's not the easiest person to work with. It's something I can't do now as I've promised not to mention it again."

"Okay. Just tell him I'm always here should he change his mind."

"Oh, definitely."

"Ashley, I like Connor. No airs and graces. He is his own person and does not pretend to be someone or something else. This is important when publicly sharing information anywhere, wedding or otherwise." He went on to explain how personality fits with speeches.

Persona

The audience will very quickly recognise if you are being anything other than authentic and genuine, so be yourself. If you do not normally tell jokes, don't do it here—you risk the joke and everything else may fall flat. Steer clear of smutty comments. Although some guests may be amused, others may be offended. Be humorous, but if you don't normally tell jokes, don't tell jokes! Speak naturally and with spontaneity.

If you learn your speech off by heart, it will most probably sound so, and will lack a natural feel about it. Use your own personality.

A wedding can be an emotional event. You will be emotional and so will others. Many people present will be married or getting married or will make links with another wedding, possibly their own, their daughter's or their son's. Your speech will be taking their minds back or forward to any of those events. Love and passion will be in the air. They will be feeling emotional for you, as well. So use your own emotions, be passionate in the way you speak and the types of things you say. Your listeners will feel this, respond and almost certainly get emotional. This will help everyone remember what you say.

Ask yourself: What were people doing while I was speaking? Were they laughing, crying, smiling, nodding

their heads? They would have been reading your NVC (non-verbal communication). What did you read from theirs? Did I get emotional and what was the reaction to this? If there was a reaction, you have been successful. Ask yourself, was I being natural? Did I sound spontaneous? Was I being me? Was I using my personality?'

Reg followed up with, "As Connor is not coming and you have pretty much finalised your words, let's deal with the next pea now."

"I'm up for that. I've got the time."

"In that case, cast your mind back to my shed wall and to the pictures. Which do you think ought to be next?" Although Ashley had been inside the shed a couple of times, he still hadn't looked around thoroughly and taken them all in, but did his best. So, he focused as best he could, on all the various pictures of peas; large peas, little peas, peas in pods, pods on their own and pea plants.

"Okay. So many pictures of peas. I'm not totally sure, but my guess is that having got the script just about right I ought to be practising how to deliver it."

"You're on target. Yes, I'd now advocate moving onto the practical side of delivering the words. It continues the preparation stage."

Ashley acknowledged this, "Magic, we're really getting down to it. This is the bit that most of us find the most frightening. The getting up in front of all those guests to speak, that is."

"Spot on. I'll keep using more of my peas to help you to be totally successful."

Ashley again imagined the walls in the posh end of the shed, found an appropriate pea and now made his own contribution, "So, come on let's get on and make some..." he drew a breath and said, "progress."

"That's right Ashley. You really have caught on pretty quickly! You've got your words scripted out. Now, really own them. Start by finding a quiet place to practise without interruptions. No noise, no TV, no others around so you can concentrate on the delivery. It's important that you remain standing for this and present the words to yourself out loud, facing a mirror—a full-length mirror if you have one."

"We've got one in the main bedroom."

"Good. At this stage, get used to looking at yourself while presenting the speech. Do it just once or twice a day for a couple of days and notice what you're doing with your hands, your head, your feet, in fact, everything. Your whole body. The reason for this is to get used to what you look like to other people and consider how others might interpret your body behaviour. Be conscious of what you are doing with your whole body, from fingertip to fingertip and from the top of your head to the soles of your feet. Keep that behaviour positive. There you go, tick off another one."

"Done."

"Another bit of research suggests that we communicate more with our bodies than with the words that come from our mouths. This is non-verbal communication or body language."

Ashley suddenly had a flashback to the first time he had seen Sophie in the reception area of the hotel in Spain. He did not have to speak with her initially to decide that he liked her. Reg was right. They communicated without speaking. He understood the concept of non-verbal communication but had never thought about it as much as Reg was causing him to do now. He recalled Reg had said something about raising the consciousness a couple of weeks earlier. We do many things without thinking, unconsciously. It was now time to move on and do things on more of a conscious level.

Reg continued, "Ashley, you're now beginning to own your speech, so prepare like this right up to the moment that your speech starts on the wedding day. And consider this, all the skills and techniques that you end up using can and will be transferred into your professional life. So give this NVC business some serious thought."

"Now, there's a coincidence. You mentioned some of that before, and I was thinking about it while waiting for you to answer the phone. The owning of the words element. Thanks for reminding me."

Sure enough, that is exactly what Ashley did. He left Reg buzzing with this information. He liked Reg's peas approach as it helped him remember the various techniques.

At lunchtime, he left his office and went to a cafe to get something to eat. He was suddenly conscious of his whole body, wondering what other people were reading into his body behaviour. Did they think him friendly, or otherwise? Did they see him as a happy or unhappy person?

He smiled to himself and felt a tingle of relaxation run right through his body. "Strange that," he thought to himself. "All I've done is become conscious of what I'm doing physically. What I'm doing with my body. I wonder what Sophie thought of me when she first saw me. Before we spoke with each other. What was her impression of me?"

Physical

Be animated. The audience will be watching your body as much as listening to the words you say—reading your body language. In conversation, we use gestures naturally.

We use our hands and move about a little. This is far more interesting and normal than standing perfectly still. Be physical. Remember, we are being judged by our body language and the verbal language we use. Just as eye contact is essential, ensure your body is facing or looking at the listeners. Be aware of what you are doing with your body and the effect it may have on the audience.

Ask yourself: What sort of body language was I using? Was it in tune with the words I used? What effect was it having on the listeners?

Later that day, Ashley was at home alone, thinking about presenting the words to himself. He was standing in the kitchen, just as Reg had suggested, but it felt really odd. Sort of uncomfortable, self-conscious, and awkward. He could not shake the feeling of being watched. He had to tell himself that it was just his imagination and that no one could possibly see or hear him. He would usually look into the mirror every morning while washing and shaving, so, what was the difference? With his tablet in hand, he began reading, "Good afternoon, everyone. My wife and I..." Just a few words into the speech the telephone rang. It was Reg with some extra information.

"Reg! I was just about to practise for the first time."

"Sorry, Ashley. I did not want to overburden you earlier. However, before you start presenting those words do what most professional sports people or actors do. They rehearse mentally. Footballers do it before a penalty shot or a free kick. Golfers do it before taking a shot such as teeing off. You've seen it yourself on TV and at live matches and games. Actors spend a substantial period rehearsing before they perform live in front of an audience."

Ashley had worked himself up to read his words out loud, and the interruption had made him a little terse with Reg. "Come on, Reg. It sounds like there's more. Get to the point, please, so I can get back to reading the words out loud for the first time."

"That's keenness. In that case, it's a good job I called now. I know you have chosen the venue for the wedding reception. Have you been in the room that it will take place?"

"Yes, we went last weekend. A neat, cosy place. A hotel where we are having the ceremony and an adjacent barn for the reception. The barn is a beautifully refurbished 16th-century building, apparently built by Henry the Eighth's carpenter. A real wow-factor place."

"Good. You're halfway there. Okay. Before you do anything else then—a big tip—do this right now. With your eyes wide open, imagine being at your reception in that barn. Imagine standing there with Sophie seated next to you and look out from where you will be speaking. See

your mum. See your dad. Look out at everyone in turn at their tables. See your friend's faces. Notice how smart they all are. They're all looking back at you. Smile and take your time. I hope you're doing this right now as I speak."

"Yes, I am."

"Good. Imagine the emotions that will be running through your body. Feel that excitement. Feel the passion. See everyone smiling back at you. Got it?"

"Yes, so what is all this about?"

"The brain doesn't know the difference between practice through imagining and the real thing. So when these sports people and actors use their imagination in this way, visualising a few times before the important action, then get to the real thing, the brain believes it's performed the action many times. It's the equivalent of real practice shots. Do the same as they do. Then, while you are practising the delivery of the words, imagine you are speaking to all those guests at the wedding reception. Continue to see their faces looking at you. Got that?"

"Yes. Can I get on with it now? I've got ninety or so people sitting in front of me waiting for my next words, and you are keeping them waiting."

"Sorry about interrupting you, but it's important."

The conversation finished, Ashley remained in his kitchen visualising; seeing and feeling everything Reg had just spoken about. He thought to himself, "Wow! I can actually see them in my mind's eye. This is really like having a conversation with all our guests, and it's making it so much easier."

It was so much easier! He really did enjoy talking to his guests. As he finished, he felt less self-conscious. He went upstairs and did it all over again, but this time he spoke to his guests via the full-length mirror. This felt weird at first. However, using his imagination, things became easier. The weirdness subsided. As he started to get into the flow of speaking, it became even easier. He really did feel as if he was talking to his guests right there in front of him.

A minor thing, but he noticed that his shirt was not tucked into his trousers properly and that his hair was a mess and started to wonder how the guests looking at him might interpret this. Would they consider that he did not care about his appearance and therefore not care about what he was saying, or could it be read as a lack of care towards the audience?

There was a realisation that we never know what is going through the minds of our observing listeners. At one stage, he realised that he could not see his face in the mirror. Why? Well, he was holding the tablet too high up, and the audience would not be able to see his face and facial expressions.

He knew that probably the most important feature of non-verbal communication is ensuring that the face is in tune with the words coming out of the mouth. Making the wrong expression at the wrong time could be read by someone as insincerity.

He then said out loud, "Wow! This is powerful."

Reg's Podcast

"Real progress can be made by practising your own speech out loud to a full-length mirror while watching your own non-verbal communication to check how other people see you. While doing so, use your imagination and visualise the guests looking at you, smiling, getting emotional. Feel those emotions, rehearsing in the way that actors and sports people do before important performances. Practising in this way while using the imagination is powerfully positive.

It's all part of the preparation."

Chapter Seven—How Do I Do This and Get It Right?

The important little chats Ashley had with family members helped him realise that turning up on the day of the wedding was only one of his responsibilities. On one occasion he was talking with his dad and future father-in-law. "Howard, thanks to you and Gwen, Reg has been guiding me towards a meaningful speech."

Gerry was the first to speak, "That's good to hear, son. Gwen mentioned something about his method. It sounds quite different, quite interesting."

"Why don't you come along to see and hear for yourself, Dad?"

"As interesting as it sounds, remember, I've been giving presentations all my professional life and will cope with my little bit without Reg. It might be handy, however, if you can pass on to me some of what he shares with you." Ashley just nodded his head while Gerry continued. "As father of the groom, my responsibilities, as far as the speeches are concerned, are very limited. That said, it's Howard here who has a greater responsibility."

Howard was standing rather sheepishly, just staring into space as he leant backwards slightly. He was as quiet as a mouse, just like his wife, and needed a bit of encouragement to speak. Gerry said, "I've declared my hand, Howard. How about you? There are three people who normally speak. In reverse order, the best man, the groom and you, the father of the bride. You are usually first to speak. You are in effect, the warm-up artist. Well?"

Howard just continued his wide-open stare with his lips tight together as he shook his head very slowly from side to side. He was not happy. The other two stood still and waited for a response which did not come.

Ashley decided to break the silence, "Come on, Mr H. It's your daughter! You'll be giving her away, and it falls on you to be first on your feet to thank people for being there, welcome me into your family and say some really nice things about me. And your daughter, of course—the person you've known since birth. If you can slip in a bit of mickey-taking, even better. It's your wonderful and beautiful Sophie."

It took a few more seconds before Howard said, "No. No. No. Sorry, I can't do it. It's not me."

Things went very quiet before Ashley asked tentatively, "Are you serious, H?"

He spoke very slowly, deliberately, "I've never been more serious in all my life. I. We. Gwen and I, that is, love our daughter to bits, but to get up in front of all those people... Sorry guys, I can't do it."

The other two stood in disbelief, neither knowing what to say. A father of the bride who would not be speaking at his only daughter's wedding? Unthinkable!

Howard looked at the other two, tears welling up in his eyes. With a lump in his throat he said, "Sorry, I can't, no, I just can't," he drew a deep breath inwards, then out came, "and won't."

Ashley could not believe his ears, "Do Sophie and Gwen know?"

Howard was now sobbing into a hankie, "I've already said sorry and explained this to Sophie. Gwen already knew how I feel about this. Neither of them are happy about it, but have accepted it."

It was Ashley who made the first move by putting his arms around Howard in a massive hug and spoke gently, "Look, H, I'm not the one to talk anyone into doing this. But, are you really sure?"

It was difficult, but Howard managed to speak, "One hundred percent positive and there's nothing anyone can do or say that will change my mind. Even the thought of it frightens the life out of me."

The trio stood looking at each other. Not a word was spoken for what seemed like a lifetime. Eventually, Howard managed to get a few more words out, "Sorry to have landed this on you. Look, I'm embarrassed and need to leave straight away." The tears were now running down the cheeks of his face. "I'll be in touch with you again when I've got over this." In complete silence, he shook hands awkwardly with them, turned, walked away, and went straight home.

Ashley and Gerry discussed what they had just heard. The conversation ended with Ashley saying, "Well Dad, it looks like you will be the warm-up act then."

Gerry's eyes opened wider than wide and, surprised look on his face, said, "Looks that way, doesn't it? It's a big, big problem that means I become the first to speak as both dads."

Within ten minutes they left and went home.

Ashley wanted to discuss what had just happened with Reg. He needed to know if there was anything that would make Howard change his mind or support him through his difficulty. Fortunately, they were meeting the next day so left it till then. "So what do you think Reg? Is there anything you can suggest that you or we can do?"

Reg rubbed his chin and looked up at the ceiling of his shed. "I've met Howard through knowing Gwen and her activities with the gardening club. Don't know him that well, but I'm willing to give him a call for a chat. Whatever you do, don't put him under pressure to speak. Leave it to me."

"Fine. You're the one with experience in this area. He's all yours."

Up to this point, Ashley had done exactly what his coach had explained to him and now felt really good about his achievements. "Moving on, then. From my point of view, this public speaking business is not as hard as I had previously thought. It's a matter of being organised, having a plan, being prepared, and mixing all that with practice and the confidence which comes from the other elements."

"That's it. Remember the peas. Keep them coming like that."

"Oh! And in my case, a little bit of help from you! Professional help from someone who knows what they are talking about. Now I must share some of the information with my dad and, if possible, my best man to ensure they're going to be successful."

Reg nodded, "Agreed. It's not as hard as people think. It's a matter of realising that the only difference between this public speaking business, as you call it, and having a normal conversation is that usually, more people are watching and listening to you. Now, having spent a couple of days practising to your visualised audience in the chosen wedding location via your mirror, you are probably wondering what's next."

"Yes, I am. Before we move on, though, that visualisation stuff has been good. Really glad you interrupted me when you did because that bit made it a lot easier to stand and speak. It was better than just looking into the mirror at myself assessing what the audience may have been seeing. I was actually seeing them in my mind's eye."

"Good. I'll tell you what you look and sound like for real when we get round to having a live session together closer to the big day. For the time being, however, we'll stick to your notes. Do you have any questions?"

"As it happens, I do. It felt a bit odd walking up to the mirror, seeing the guests and then launching into talking to them."

"Ah! Great because that leads us neatly into something I was saving till much later when we do the live practice. However, as you've brought it up, it's what many people call The Six S's of Starting a Speech. Yes, I was saving this for much later"

"The what?"

"The Six S's of Starting a Speech. It's been around for ages. Don't know its origin."

"Come on Reg. The peas of public speaking, the BBC of structure and now these S's. How many more of these acronym things are there? Oh! Then there's Connor's addition of brussels, broccoli and carrots."

"Yes, that tickled me as well. The truth is, Ashley, there are quite a few more. They help us remember the different techniques. Give this some thought. Consider what we are doing together with the peas and other information.

We are working through the equivalent of a two or three-day professional public speaking course I used to deliver before retiring last year. I now do it for individuals like you with a special need—like your wedding."

Ashley could not contain himself, "Yeah, okay. Let's get on with the S for spinach." He could not hold that in and felt a bit cocky, like Connor, for a few moments.

"Oh, how droll! The truth is, Ashley, there are quite a few more. As I've said, they help us remember the different techniques. Right. The Six S's. Imagine this: you're sitting and waiting to be introduced to do your bit. It's a bit of an extension to preparing like the actor and sportsperson we spoke about previously. Do this and not only will you be relaxed, but the whole audience will also be waiting with anticipation. It goes like this; Sit, Stand, Silence, Smile, Scan—then, and only then—Speak."

"Hang on. You mean to tell me that just by be being quiet and smiling everyone will respond and I will feel more relaxed?"

"Most definitely, Ashley. Even more so if you take a deep breath or two while doing it. We'll talk more about the power of silence in due course, but for the time being, let me tell you something about my wife. She, like me, has retired from mainstream work now. I do this, and she's still involved in the Girlguiding movement. Anyway, just imagine being in a big hall with twenty or so excited young girl guides, all having fun, when one of the leaders wants to get their attention. Shouting is okay, but that would be noise over the top of noise. So, what they do is remain totally silent and raise one arm high in the air. One by one, the girls see that arm and each of them raises one of their own arms. In no time at all, the whole room is completely quiet with everyone holding one arm up in the air and looking at the leader. The leader gains everyone's complete attention. I've seen her get more than 200 to fall silent at a major Girlguiding event, just by raising her arm. I've used it myself many, many times in different settings such as classrooms, when working with youngsters in schools and even at the gardening club's committee meetings. The difference here in your case is rather than using silence and your arm, you just use silence, a smile and the scanning of your eyes. It's part of the amazing power of silence."

"Yeah. Yeah. I can just see that happening down the social club at closing time."

"Get Billy the bar manager to try it sometime. I think you'll be surprised at the effect."

Reg needed to move on, "Most of the time we have been covering the what and now it's time to deal more deeply with the how—what to deliver and now how to deliver it. Remember, the next time you present to your audience in the mirror use The Six S's first. And breathe."

Ashley repeated The Six S's, "Sit, stand, silence, smile, scan, speak. Hey! Simple."

"Very good. Now, any other queries?"

"No. Not about what I have experienced so far. I just want to know about the next pea."

"Okay. It's to do with your notes—précis. Up to now, you have been practising while referring to a script which stretches over several pages. This is all very well, initially, but if you do this during the wedding you'll be tempted to read some of the scripted words, and that may make you sound rather unnatural and lifeless. The aim is to sound natural and spontaneous, as if in normal conversation—nice and relaxed."

"I was trying that, but couldn't get it. How do I get over that?"

"By now, you should know your speech content quite well. Before you start to learn it off by heart cut the script down from all those pages to a short list. Bullet points which will act as reminders of what you intend to say."

There was slight panic in Ashley's voice and face, "Hang on. That's where I started. With a list. Anyway, I will need my script."

"That initial list was the bare bones of ideas to get you started, and then you added the flesh. That enabled you to work out exactly what to say. Now you only need a short list to trigger the extended information. It will be a completely different list. Speaking from this you will sound far more natural and spontaneous. Sorry, but you don't need the full script."

Ashley was not panicking but was certainly getting a little concerned. He took a moment and thought about it. Then, "Hang on, I've gone along with everything so far and been quite successful, so there's no harm giving this a try I suppose. If I don't like it though, I'll be going back to the full script. Tell me what to do and how to do it."

"Go home and sit down with your script as it is now and read it through. Then, highlight all the main points and practise the speech to the mirror. But this time only refer to the highlighted bits. Do that a few times over the next couple of days just as you have been doing with the full script."

"Is that it?"

"Not quite. When that's done, and you're sure that all the main points have been highlighted, transfer them onto one piece of paper, a single card or new document. Create your bullet point list. Then present out loud to yourself again: only use those words from this list as a reminder. They'll help you remember what to say. If you watch something like BBC Parliament on the telly, you'll see some of the politicians with a small piece of paper giving, in some cases, a lengthy speech. It's their abbreviated list, their aide-mémoire. Some write the précised list on the palm of their hand, so no paper is held at all."

Précis

Reading from a script sounds unnatural so think about cutting it down. There is always a risk that by holding a full script at the event you will read it rather than use it to remind you of the speech's content. You will reach a stage when the full script is known so well you can reduce it down to a list of bullet points. Initially, work through the script, highlight the main points, and practise the delivery from the highlighted selection only. Then cut the script into short notes or bullet points using the highlighted pieces.

Continue practising the delivery from this list as an aide-mémoire. You will sound far more spontaneous.

Ask yourself: Is the list sufficient to prompt me? Can I cut it even further? Do I need notes at all?

Reg then mentioned a couple of examples. "David Cameron spoke at a Conservative Party conference for about 45 minutes without notes. He had practised those words so many times he knew exactly what he wanted to say and they came across very spontaneously. When Chris Froome won his second Tour de France, he stood on the winner's podium with a small piece of paper. His short, emotional speech was broadcast worldwide, and he only looked down at the paper a couple of times. Recently, he spoke without any notes at all. He's getting more confident and experienced."

"I heard about Cameron. Didn't see him. But I did see Froome. He's one of my cycling heroes."

Practice

Once the full script has been established, you need to practise speaking the words out loud, preferably to a trusted individual who is sworn to secrecy. However, before that, read the script to yourself in your head. Then progress to reading out loud while standing and facing a full-length mirror. This will help you assess what you look like to those who will be watching and listening to you. The process of reading out loud, eventually to somebody else, will help you tweak the text with fresh ideas.

Ask yourself: What do I look like? How do I feel? Are my words in tune with my body language? How might I make the delivery better?

"And while you're practising, start timing yourself. Make sure you don't exceed the length of time allocated for you to speak at the reception. Every speaker needs to have a time slot that fits in with the caterers. The last thing anyone wants is for the meal to get cold while you are all speaking. Remember, I would recommend that each speaker gets about ten to fifteen minutes each, dependent upon how much time you're allocating overall and how much time is available. You may find that the best man will possibly need more time than the others."

"Good point. We've also got to decide when the speeches are going to be. Before or after the meal. One after another or between courses? More decisions."

"That's got to be it for this session. I'm off for my midweek swim. And remember, practise, practise, practise! You will only give this speech once so put every effort into it. Make it memorable for the right reasons."

They parted. Reg enjoyed his exercise while Ashley travelled home, still contemplating his next tasks. On reaching home, he and Sophie discussed her father's decision and the tasks that Reg had set for him.

He decided not to do anything else that day but left his brain to work overnight. He thought to himself, "Not sure about this précis business and creating a bullet point list."

Three peas stuck out in his mind. Practise, practise, practise. This was the last thing he thought of before going to sleep.

Reg's Podcast

"Once the full script is how you want it, cut it down by highlighting the main points. Then cut it again into bullet points and practise from there. Practise to a mirror out loud and notice how others see you.

The mantra of the day has got to be practise, practise, practise.

Remember to make it memorable for the right reasons."

Chapter Eight—The First Live Practice

Practise, practise, practise! Reg's final words stuck with Ashley as he drifted off to sleep and yes, he agreed with them. He recognised this speech was so important that great effort needed to be put into it so that it was memorable for the right reasons. On waking the next morning, Ashley was thinking preparation, preparation, preparation. He also enjoyed a light-bulb moment, "I now know the story to tell during the speech." It amazed him how the brain seemed to keep working during sleep and that fresh ideas were there waiting for him on waking up. "I should just ask myself a question before my head hits the pillow and the answer will often be there when I wake up."

"You're later than usual, Ash." Sophie welcomed Ashley home after work later that day. "I bet you've been down the gym."

"Yes, but not to do any fitness training today."

Sophie was intrigued, "Been to the gym but not there to exercise. Are you okay? Meeting a chum? Is there something wrong with you?"

"Look, my head is still in a spin from completing the work Reg gave me. Let's have dinner and talk after that."

Sophie could see he was a bit on the tired side, so she agreed. In fact, they talked about the gym visit meeting during dinner. "During my lunch break, I went into a small quiet office with my script and began highlighting those key points. The whole hour was taken up doing it. On the way home, I nipped into the gym as I knew it would be quiet before the evening rush. I managed to get into an empty exercise studio, where there are several full-length mirrors, with the new highlighted version of the speech. From that, I delivered the speech facing the mirrors. It wasn't easy, but practise, practise, practise kept coming back to me. I knew it was worth the effort. Only ran through the notes twice and must admit I needed to refer to the full version a few times. Still, I'm really pleased with myself."

Sophie was impressed by the amount of effort he was putting into it and gave him a smacking, great kiss. She knew how important it was to them both and to everyone attending the wedding.

"Well done, darling. Even though I don't know what you're going to say I'm sure it will be really good. Your effort will be worth it."

Necessary arrangements were made with Reg for the next meeting. They would meet at Ashley's home on the following Saturday morning, when the speech would be delivered live to Reg. He would have preferred to have Ashley give the speech at the wedding venue, but it was being used for another event. Ashley did not want Sophie to be there, so asked her to pop round to see her mum— which is exactly what she did.

By the time Saturday morning arrived, Ashley had précised the highlighted version down to the shortened aide-mémoire. As soon as Reg arrived he said, "Right, let's get straight to it. You deliver the speech to me here while imagining all your guests are also here right in front of you. So not just to me, but every single person. Just the way I explained before and the way you should've been putting things into practice."

Both Ashley and Reg then sat on chairs at opposite ends of the room. "Remember The Six S's Ashley, glance down at your précised notes only when really necessary. Right, let me introduce you as if I'm your best man, Connor, who you said may act as master of ceremonies on the day."

"Connor? I'm not so sure about that. If he can't prepare a speech, how can we expect him to be the MC as well? How about this Reg," Ashley interrupted, "You were, are, a Toastmaster. You are now officially invited with your wife to the wedding, and you can officiate if you would like to. What do you think?"

"Well, that is very kind of you Ashley. I'll speak to Silvia and look at the diary. Thank you very much."

"Magic. I'll speak with Sophie and her mum to get you on the list and arrange the invites."

"I'll still need to check with my wife, though. Let's get back to where we were then. An introduction, 'Ladies and gentlemen it gives me very great pleasure to introduce to you the man responsible for making Sophie so happy today and for apparently causing such a fuss on his stag do, which you will almost certainly hear about when Connor presents his best man's speech. I give you the bridegroom, Ashley.' Give it a few seconds for the applause and possibly some heckling from your close friends. Take your time. There is no hurry."

Still seated at the other end of the room, Ashley then said to himself, "Sit, stand, silence, smile, scan," and followed those instructions. He looked around the room visualising his wife, family and friends and hearing them applauding. As he began number six—speaking—he saw them all smiling back at him. All Six S's covered. He then delivered the speech to his happy audience using the précised notes from his tablet.

"Wow, Ashley my friend! For a first, proper delivery to someone. That was pretty impressive. Give yourself a massive pat on the back. I loved those stories. There was a real aahh factor. Sophie will be surprised with them so have the tissues ready for her. In fact, it would be a good idea to have a box of tissues on each table for people to mop up the tears."

Ashley breathed a massive sigh of relief. He did not say a word for about a minute, and then, "I must admit I was not looking forward to that, Reg, but now it's done I feel quite chuffed. You're right, the preparation and practice have been worth it. Now, please, give me some feedback."

"Okay, give yourself a few minutes. Take a drink of water and settle for a while and rather than me speak first, you tell me what you thought of your performance."

After a couple of minutes, Ashley got his thoughts together and commented on his delivery to Reg.

"That was a fair assessment, Ashley. I've got a couple of comments. However, rather than overburden you with information now, I'm going to give you a document for you to read at your leisure. Couple the details in this with all the bits and pieces we have discussed over recent weeks."

"So, now what?"

"Okay. The only feedback I'm going to give you at this stage relates to one of the words that will feature in that document. It's a list of fifteen peas. Each of them relates to one of the tips for successful public speaking and each is associated with my peas."

"Which one are you going to highlight?"

"Here's the document. Before you read the note, you were smiling at the outset. Were you smiling throughout?"

"Possibly not."

"Definitely not. Can you offer a reason why you were not smiling?"

"Well, all I can think of is that I was probably concentrating so hard on the words. Remember I've not done anything like this before and it was from the new list. Maybe the next live practice will be different."

"Yes. That look of concentration and whatever you feel like will disappear with a bit more of this type of live practice. Take a look at the sheet and read the pea about pleasant which relates to smiling and see how anything there fits."

Reg handed him the sheet and Ashley read the pea for pleasant to himself.

Pleasant

It is essential to look and feel good, so smile. Remember, you will have started out with The Six S's which include a smile, be pleasant, be pleasing, be personable throughout. This will help you relax and look more appealing and friendly to the guests. It is like looking in a mirror and smiling—the smile is returned to you. It is the same with an audience, smile and they will smile back. Smiling also has a relaxing effect on you. This is real communication. Remember, "Smile, and the whole world smiles with you."

Ask yourself: Did I smile? What was the reaction from the audience? How did it make me feel?

After reading this section, Ashley gave a knowing nod and gentle smile, "Yes, I get it. I take the point about it being similar to the smile in The Six S's. So turning this on its head, if I look out at my listeners with a grumpy face, the chances are they will mirror that back to me."

"Almost certainly. And once they're in that mood, the chances are they'll stay that way even once you realise it and begin smiling again. It's difficult to claw it back."

"Smile. Now, I take it that I only smile when appropriate. As it is a happy occasion, I'll almost certainly be in a happy mood and therefore have an appropriate, pleasant look on my face."

"That's right. When speaking at another time on a different topic, your face has to be in tune with that topic. When mentioning absent friends in the speech, depending on the circumstances of their absence, it may not be appropriate to smile. Watch the newscasters on the telly and how they change their expressions to suit the news item they are talking about."

Ashley looked down at the sheet given to him, "Thanks. I'll do that. These questions at the bottom of the pleasant section?"

"They are there to offer a bit of guidance as to the type of questions you ought to be asking yourself after the delivery. It helps you assess your level of smiling and the effect it had. There are similar self-checking questions after each of the tips."

"Mmmm. Seems sound enough to me. I need to look at the other letters as well, then."

"Not now. Consider each of them and apply them as you practise delivering the speech. You can also use them to help assess your delivery."

He pointed out that these tips were about presentation delivery, and that this was not a "top tips" list, just fifteen tips. "We've already dealt with some of these tips while others are new to you. The list brings them all together."

Ashley responded positively, "Magic. I'll have a proper look at this when I get home."

"Yes, it's best to do it at home as there is quite a bit of information to take in. That said, I will also offer some more feedback along with a suggestion. That story leading up to the giving of the present to Sophie ought to be paced a bit slower and have more pauses in it. This will build up the suspense for everyone present, your guests and especially Sophie. See the pea for pace and pause later in the list. Whatever you now do with it, do not tell anyone what you intend to say. Keep it a total surprise for everyone. My lips are definitely sealed."

Pace & Pause

A speech is not a race. Take your time. There is no rush, unless a sit-down meal is pending. Work out exactly how much time you have and ensure the speech sticks to it. Remember, there are points in the speech where you will need to slow down or speed up for emphasis. Also, allow time for people to laugh, cheer or cry, so slow down or stop talking to let them do this. Consider a pause occasionally. It is good for you to catch a breather. Take a drink of water (not alcohol). It is also useful to use pauses just as silence is used at the beginning (The Six S's) to get people's attention. Use this technique to maintain everyone's attention throughout the body, especially at points where you want them to really take note of what you are saying, what you are about to say or have just said. Trust the power of silence.

Ask yourself: How did I use pace and pause? Did I use the power of silence? How did I apply pace? What was the reaction?

Ashley smiled with pleasure, "Thanks. Sophie's mum and dad know about the story as they gave me the idea. They do not know about the present, though, nor how I intend giving it to her. That's the bit that'll surprise everyone and be super memorable. There you are, you've got me using the word now."

Reg was as pleased as Ashley, "Fantastic."

And finally…

They had already covered these next two peas, but Reg included them to ensure Ashley fully appreciated their importance. To do so, he used a story to build a picture in his mind. To cover story, Reg uses the pea word parable. This is how it went.

"A few years back, in a general election speech, the leader of the Labour Party, Tony Blair, said that when Labour was elected back into government, he would place emphasis on three very important topics of national importance. Whenever he said this in speeches there would then be a pause for effect to give his audience a few moments to think—then he would say 'Education, education, education'. There was always a slight pause between each of the three words. Extremely effective.

However, in the case of public speaking those top topics are –

Preparation – Preparation – Preparation
and
Practise – Practise – Practise"

Ashley nodded his head in agreement, "Interesting that, as I've been thinking about those words quite a bit. I've heard that Winston Churchill put a great deal of effort into preparing for and practising his speeches. That's probably why he sounded so good. So natural."

Reg added, "Likewise, great comedians put hours and hours of preparation into their performances before delivering their material. Now there is an example of timing—pace and pause—making so much difference to the delivery."

Parable

The entertainer Max Bygraves used to say, "I wanna tell you a story." Then he would take the listener on a journey of fun, laughter, and emotions all leading up to a humorous conclusion, the punchline. Think of contemporary comedians who go beyond telling jokes by telling a tale relating to a real-life experience or situation to build up to their punchline or conclusion. People love stories or anecdotes. The storyteller is doing more than just speaking words. Stories help the listener paint pictures in their own mind based on the speaker's words and associated gestures.

Consider also using props to help bring the stories to life.

Ask yourself: How effective were my stories? What reaction was I getting? Could I produce some real pictures that will bring my words to life? How about the use of other props?

They put another date in their diaries for Ashley to deliver the speech again to Reg. With the amount of work carried out so far, the next delivery would almost certainly be the last to Reg before the wedding.

Ashley accompanied Reg to the front door and, as they shook hands, he said, "Millions of thanks, Reg. With

all the information you've shared with me and the success I've achieved, I feel that both Connor and Howard would benefit from a few words of encouragement."

"Look, please leave Howard to me. Since you told me about Howard's reluctance to speak at the wedding, I've had a word with him on the phone. At this time, there is no positive movement, but I would never say never."

"Fine. I'll accept your judgement on Howard but must have another chip at Connor."

Ashley settled down in his lounge with his copy of the fifteen tips. Sophie arrived home shortly after, and he shared with her what had happened. "I'm really pleased it is going well for you Ashley. Yes, leave my dad to Reg, and good luck with Connor."

Reg's Podcast

"As often as I say it and will continue to repeat it, there is no substitute: practise, practise, practise! While doing so, take account of where and when emphasis needs to be put on the words and phrases used. Those three peas hold equal standing with preparation, preparation, preparation.

Get the pace right by speeding up and slowing down to hold the attention of the audience. Also, use the power of silence, especially before and after important bits of the speech. This allows the audience time to think about what is about to be said or what has just been said.

The list of peas is key to all speeches.

Be pleasant. 'Smile and the whole world smiles with you.'"

Chapter Nine—Coordinating the Speaking Performances

Although Ashley had stuck to his word and not mentioned to Connor anything about his speech, he had been updating him on what he and Reg had been discussing. There were now other things that needed to be talked about. Ashley had decided to put speaking with Connor off for a couple of days so he could focus on revising his highlighted script and continue précising it into bullet points.

Sophie offered some advice, "Make sure you see him soon. The stag is not that far away now, and he needs to be reminded again how important this is."

"Yes, but I am going to be gentle with him. Although he is reluctant, I need to speak to the others who want to speak on our big day, so everything is coordinated. I bet he hasn't done anything about that, either."

"So who's on the final list?"

"There's Connor, of course. Reg will deal with your dad. I know my dad wants to speak. That's it for the reception. Then there's Toby and Abbie, who will be speaking at the ceremony."

"Anyone else?"

"Well, I think there might be another who just might want to..." He tailed off and stopped speaking.

There was a silence while she waited for a name. "Come on, who?"

"There's traditional speeches, and then there's our wedding speeches."

"What are you saying?"

"How do you fancy our wedding being a little different? How do you fancy having someone break with tradition?" There was a pause before he asked the next question very slowly. "How do you fancy being a bride who speaks at her own wedding?"

The subsequent silence made it obvious that Sophie had been surprised. Yet, Sophie's face hinted that she might have a surprise in store herself.

"Tradition. Our wedding? Me, the bride, speaking? Doing it differently? Well," another silence, "Do you realise you've gone and spoilt it?"

Ashley was a little mystified, "Spoilt what?"

"Look. You said it yourself. Be different. Now, this is between you and me. It was going to be a surprise, and I want it to remain that way. A surprise to everyone else. The truth is, I've been talking with a friend who broke with tradition and spoke on her own big day. She absolutely loved it, and so did her guests. Apparently, her parents were in tears of joy over it."

Ashley developed a massive beamer of a smile and said, "And you've been chatting with her about surprising everyone, including me, by speaking at the wedding. Oh, that's fantastic. I love you, Sophie. This is going to be such a magical event. I'm so pleased you want to do this. And there was me thinking you might hesitate, put me off, or say no."

"Well, you were wrong mister big shot Ashley Jamison. The future Mrs Jamison already knew that more and more brides were speaking at their weddings. It's almost becoming expected. But please, you mustn't tell anyone else."

Ashley had no option but to agree. Huddled together on the sofa, they carried on talking about it for a while. Then, they planned how to get all the prospective speakers together to get arrangements settled. "Things are getting a bit urgent now, Sophie. I suggest we get this sorted this week." Ashley was now talking with quiet excitement.

Later in the week, they both got together at their home with Connor, Toby, and Abbie. Things started off with a nice little chat about what each had been doing recently before they eventually got round to talking about the wedding and, more specifically, the speeches.

"Okie-Dokie. Let's update on the speeches and make some plans. Let's KISS this." There were some surprised faces at this.

Toby, tongue-in-cheek, said, "The only one I'm going to kiss is my mum, and you should only be kissing Sophie."

"Sorry. It's something Reg said in the coaching. By KISS I mean I want to keep this as short and simple as possible. And definitely to the point."

As the laughter subsided, Ashley continued, "Reg suggests applying the kiss principle to speeches: keep it simple, keep it short and sweet. Let's do that tonight as well."

Connor, in his usual devil-may-care manner, said, "Good grief, bruv! And so the list gets larger. Before, there was that brussels, broccoli, and carrots thingy and now this KISS business. He's really got inside you, hasn't he? It's twaddle, matey!"

Plain

There is no need to complicate things, so use the KISS principle (keep it simple or keep it short and sweet). Keep everything to the plain and simple essentials. Tell a short story or an anecdote, but if you keep it to the point, it will be far more effective and memorable! Avoid jargon and keep everything said and done, inclusive. Use props whenever possible to enhance and support your words.

Ask yourself: Was it KISSed? Did I KISS? Did I? How long was it? Did I keep it to time? Did I include everyone?

Ashley was a little frustrated by Connor but hoped he was not showing it. "I know you don't like the theory side of what he and I have been discussing, but there is a great deal of merit in it. Before we finish, I will share something else from him."

Connor could not resist saying something, "Give me patience. And I bet it's yet another one of these acronymie, whatsit thingies."

"You're not quite right, Connor. But it's full of hints and tips about speaking in public like the one's you're spending all your energy avoiding."

Connor had to go for it again, "Lordy. Lordy. Lordy. All this, just for a simple wedding speech. If I ever get wed, there won't be any speeches, if this is what we have to go through."

"Ah, but this is mine and Sophie's wedding, and you are part of it as my best man. Just for once, please take it seriously! It may seem like a one-off for you, but you never know when this twaddle may come in useful in the future."

"Well, you already know what I'm doing about my speech. For the benefit of Abbie and Toby, I'll be sorting mine out after the stag. Can't wait for that bit—get down to it." Then, in a raised voice, "Barcelona here we come."

Ashley had just one thing to say, "There's just no way of stopping you! Is there?"

"Nope. No changing me, matey."

Level-headed Sophie interrupted them, "Come on, you two. Let's accept that Connor will be making a speech and he will be preparing it at some stage after the stag. Connor, I hope you do it before you get up on your feet at the wedding."

Connor held his head high and as he nodded just once he had one final thing to say, "Don't you worry your little heart out. Just trust me. You wait till you see what I've got in store for you two at the end of my speech. See. I've done a little bit."

Taking the lead from Sophie, Ashley interrupted, "As the groom, I'll obviously be up on my feet. My dad will be speaking at some stage during the reception. Then," making eye contact with Toby and Abbie, "there's you two."

Abbie was quick to notice someone missing from the list, "You haven't mentioned Sophie's dad."

Sophie decided to handle this query, "Look, Dad is not a confident person, especially as a speaker. This is seriously freaking him out, so he has decided not to speak. Please do not say anything as we are all very disappointed and any discussion about it will upset me even more than I already am."

They all glanced at each other, not knowing what to say. Even Connor was unusually quiet. For a moment, anyway. Then, "Hey. Good old Howard. I've recently heard of a couple who decided not to have any speeches at all, to prevent all this hassle and anxiety. Well done H."

Ashley moved things along, "The bottom line is, we are having them. So, that brings us back to you two."

Toby then spoke on behalf of Abbie and himself, "Since being introduced to each other we've put our heads together over this and decided that I'll read something at the ceremony. While Abbie," he turned his gaze to her and while staring straight into her eyes continued, "will be reciting a poem about love and marriage at the ceremony. Hope this suits you."

"Toby, my friend, that is splendid. Absolutely spot on. Thank you both so much."

Sophie was so pleased as well, "Oh, how wonderful! Please, don't tell us anymore. Let it be a surprise."

"Tell you anymore? I don't know exactly which piece to read yet. There are four pieces I have found so far and want to pick bits out from each of them and hopefully combine into one. I'm also speaking with a celebrant friend who has offered to assist me. Can I tell them about yours, Abbie?"

Abbie spoke up, "No, I can speak for myself, thanks." Sophie noticed that, very interestingly, something was going on between the two of them. Abbie continued, "I'm writing my own poem for you. Something completely original."

Sophie was suddenly welling up, "Oh how sweet! You lovely, lovely person!" She got up out of her seat and hugged her friend.

Connor, who had been quiet for a while, felt the need to chip in and said sarcastically, "Make sure you prepare properly to prevent a poor performance."

Ashley was surprised, "So Connor. You have picked up something from Reg. His peas have affected you after all."

"Well bruv, that's all I've been hearing from you for weeks now. Reg said this. Reg said that. Reg said the other. Peas and pictures are driving me up the shed wall. Just you wait till I speak. If there is one thing I know will get a mention—it will be peas."

Ashley showed a bit of surprise, "Wow! Connor. So you have done some prep work. More than just the conclusion."

"Don't get too excited, Ashie baby. Them's the only things I've decided, and just for a laugh, I think I'll get a fancy-dress outfit and dress up as a pea pod. That'll make my presence and performance positively memorable."

Toby chipped in, "I'd love to see that. It'll be great for the photos."

Ashley was pleased with the way things were going, "Thanks you lot. This is going really well."

Connor had not finished speaking, so he asked Abbie and Toby, "Do you two want to be introduced to Reg and his shed and talk peas?"

They were both amused by Connor and his manner. Abbie said, "I'm not sure if you know this, Connor, but we are both teachers so we are quite used to speaking to large groups of people. We will take care of our own performances—we'll be doing a little bit of practising together."

Yet again, Sophie felt that something may be developing between those two. She glanced at Ashley and flicked her eyes sideways to Toby and Abbie. Ashley gave her a very subtle nod.

Ashley was keen to get on, "The other thing I want to get organised is when each person is to speak. I've only been to a handful of weddings but spoken with loads of people and listened to their experiences. It seems that the speakers, especially the last to speak," now looking directly at Connor, "have to wait so long and get all anxious and do not enjoy their meal. So, instead of the speeches all being clumped together at the end of the reception, we can have them dotted about. Maybe between the courses of food? What do you think?"

Abbie spoke, "It does not affect us two, but that sounds really sensible to me."

Connor seemed to like the suggestion as well. "So does that mean I wouldn't have to wait so long to insult and embarrass you?"

Sophie rose to the bait, "You dare spoil my day..."

Ashley quickly butted in, "It's alright, Sophie. Don't let him get to you. Well? Like the idea?"

Connor had successfully wound Sophie up. "It's fine by me. Get it done and dusted as soon as possible."

Ashley was delighted. "Right. This is my plan. Sophie and her mum have done all the liaising with the hotel wedding coordinator so far. They can arrange this with the catering staff, so they know exactly what we want. Sophie?"

"Yes. We've already floated the idea with the coordinator and now need to finalise it."

Ashley carried on, "Good. How about this? It's so simple. Assuming Howard is not speaking there are three of us to be concerned about, my dad, me and you, Connor. In that order. The master of ceremonies, whoever that ends up being, welcomes everyone and tells everyone what is happening. My dad fills the slot that the father of the bride normally takes, and he will speak shortly after we enter the barn. That will be as soon as everyone is seated and settled and before the starter. Then I go after the starter. You, Connor, can go straight after the main course."

Connor sat thinking for a moment. "Hmmm. Yeah, but that means I still have to be thinking about it right through the nosebag. I'd rather go before that, straight after you."

Ashley acknowledged this, "Must say, it does make perfect sense. I'm fine with that."

Connor said, "Okay. I'm guessing your dad will only speak for a short while."

"Yes, that's right. Five minutes, max."

"Brill, matey. Just to get this right in my head. Gerry, before the starts. You, Ashley, go after the starts, immediately followed by me, before the main bit of food."

In agreement, Ashley, said, "That way, I suppose you can enjoy your meal and not have to be thinking about it while eating and possibly spoiling your fish and chips. Yes, I'm joking about the fish and chips."

Connor was being sensible for a change as this was to his advantage. "Nothing wrong with fish and chips. Certainly memorable, especially if served with... wait for it, everyone... mushy peas." Everyone burst out laughing. "And your speeches will make it memorable by dotting them about differently."

When it calmed down, Ashley turned and looked at Sophie, "What do you think about that, darling?"

Sophie was smiling and nodding in agreement, "What, fish and chips with mushy peas? No, seriously, sound. My only concern is what happens after the meal with everyone sitting there, twiddling their thumbs with nothing to do."

Toby offered a suggestion. "I understand you have a magician coming along to entertain after dinner. Am I right?"

"Yes, you are. She is a friend of a friend. She's a comedian as well."

"Even better. Keep it plain and simple. She entertains people after dinner while they are still at their tables through coffee or whatever else you are having."

Ashley continued to be pleased the way things were progressing, "Genius. That's it. Done. Settled. Sophie, can you and your mum finalise that with the hotel so that the catering staff know what is happening and the timings?"

Connor still had his thinking cap on, "Timings?"

Ashley had to explain, "Yes. The catering people will need to know how long each of us is going to be so that the hot food doesn't get overcooked or go cold."

"Oh. Right, got it."

Ashley was getting things done now, "I'll tell my dad he'll have five minutes, maximum. I'll be about fifteen. How long do you want Connor?"

"How do I know? Nothing much planned, yet. Defo nothing written yet."

"See. See how even the simplest things impact on everything else?"

"Yeah. Yeah. Yeah. Alright. I don't know. How long does the main attraction speak for?"

Ashley made a suggestion, "How about we allocate you twenty minutes?"

"Twenty minutes? That's a blimming lifetime!"

"You are the star of the show. The main act. Everybody will be expecting to be entertained by the best man. Having said that, you aren't really the best man. I am."

Connor was now shaking his head from side to side, "Twenty flipping minutes. What am I going to nag about for so long? Let's hope a lot happens on the stag."

Sophie could not contain herself again. "Connor. You have twenty minutes, and that's final. Deal with it, man."

Ashley felt satisfied with what had been achieved in such a short space of time. "Thanks, everyone. Now that the work is done, let's grab a glass of wine."

So they did. About an hour later, Abbie said, "It's been a pleasant and productive evening everyone. It's time we were off."

It was Sophie who commented, "We?"

Abbie was quick to respond, "Yes, we live quite close to each other, so we came together."

"Anything you want to tell us?"

Abbie was very firm, "No."

They all guessed what was going on but said nothing more. Ashley broke the awkward silence by giving everyone a copy of Reg's fifteen peas. "Take it or leave it. I've found the information in this helpful. Hope you do as well."

Once the others had gone, Ashley and Sophie settled down and chatted a little while longer. "Thanks for not mentioning my short speech. Although the magician suggestion was good, maybe that's the point at which I can do my bit. Immediately after the main course. The magician can come on after me."

Ashley agreed immediately, "Done and dusted."

Sophie suddenly had one more thought though. "Ashley, there are a couple of people we've completely ignored."

He sat squinting slightly, thinking as hard as possible but could not identify anyone else. "Well, you've got me on this one, my love."

"The mums. We have not even considered the mums."

"Oops. Yes, you're right we haven't given them a thought. The truth is that we have now. No, they won't want to speak."

Sophie needed to query this assumption, "Are you sure?"

Ashley was certain, "Definitely. They will not want to and will not be speaking. We've got enough and, besides, the guests won't want to be sitting there all evening listening to all of us going on and on."

"Well, I think you ought to be polite and ask them anyway."

"I suppose they should at least be asked just in case. After all, they have played a major part in all the arrangements so far."

The pair of them settled down and eventually went off to bed.

A bit more preparation completed.

Reg's Podcast

"Many people rely on a wedding coordinator or Toastmaster to arrange such things as the speeches and coordinating their timing with the wedding venue staff. If the wedding will not include a coordinator, it is important to do it yourself. Keep it plain and simple, and get all the speakers together. Chat through the arrangements and make it clear who is going to speak, when they are speaking and for how long.

Bear in mind that nothing is perfect, so be prepared in case other things happen on the big day. Occasionally, other people not on your schedule will want to speak. Be ready for the possibility of having to change anything and everything!

The preparation phase starts early in the process and continues right up to the big day.

Remember the Scout motto: Be Prepared."

Chapter Ten—The Final Hurdles and the Final Wedding Performances

The final hurdles leading up to the wedding included the stag event in Barcelona. A few months earlier, a conversation had taken place between the happy couple and their parents along with Connor, at Sophie's home. Connor kicked it off, "Hi all. Cheers for coming to discuss my stag do in Barcelona!"

Ashley was a little shocked by this statement, "Your stag do? It's my wedding, not yours."

"Ah, yeah, but I'm arranging it, bruv. I'm the best dude. It's my job. It'll fuel my speech."

"You're arranging it? It should've been booked ages ago when we agreed on the people and the location."

All Connor could say was, "Come on my top bruv. I've been busy with other stuff."

Ashley shook his head, "You've had plenty of time. Why put things off like this? You're delaying that and your speech, now. Wait till it's my turn to be your best man, I'll get my own back."

"Ashie, matey, I've told you so many times now that I'll put some words together after the stag. I've got a few ideas, and the Barcelona gig will cement those ideas."

"Come on, then. Get on with it! What's the extra special thing you need to mention?"

"Do we all agree it will be at the hotel in Barcelona that me and Ashie boy first chose to go on holiday to, but didn't get to?"

Gerry chipped in, "I thought that was already agreed."

Howard remained in his shell and just shrugged his shoulders.

Gwen, however, had a little smug smile on her face.

Connor had a surprise suggestion for most people there. "I've been nagging away with one of the future mums-in-law, we've come up with a plan. You'll fall over in love with it."

Ashley was getting annoyed with him, yet again, "Last minute, once more! Everything was supposed to have been done, dusted, and booked."

It was Connor's turn to smile and look smug just like Gwen, "Keep your hairy bits on, bruv. Booking's not quite done. Won't be a problem. That's a mere minor formality."

Ashley could not let this go, "Just like your speech."

Then, like a bolt out of the blue, Connor struck, "Wait for it, guys." He waited a few seconds, then said, "This is staggeringly brilliant. Get it? Staggeringly!" He paused again. Nobody was amused. "A joint stag and hen do!"

Ashley was beside himself with shock. With wide-open mouth, he said, "What? Where did that come from?"

Gwen had to own up to this one. Quite excitedly, she said, "Oh, loves! I just thought it would be nice for us all to go together, you know, together. Nice for all the young boys and girls to have a bit of fun. Sophie could bring all her friends. Ashley could do the same. You know, all the boys and girls together. What fun. And the mums and dads and friends would all be together too. And then there's my friend Jilly. And Jilly's never been to Spain and… and I do like being with Jilly, and then there's…"

Sophie, like Ashley, was beside herself. "Sorry, mum. No deal. You'll have to go with Jilly on another occasion."

Ashley had the final words, "No. And that's final."

Connor tried saying something, "Come on bruv. I, we just thought…"

Ashley had some more final words, "You just thought. Well, you just thought wrong. Don't say another word about it. Get it booked for the men only. You've got the list, now do something about it."

Gwen looked around the group, then to Connor and rather sheepishly said, "It was just a thought. All being together and all that. Thanks for doing that for me, Connor."

Sophie looked to her mum, "Mum, how could you? You should've spoken to me, and I would've given you the no without this special meeting."

Connor remained totally silent, in mild embarrassment.

Ashley had the final word, "Connor. Get it done, you clown of a best man." As they were all together, they decided to move the conversation on to other wedding-related matters and they all eventually parted.

Connor booked the stag event the following day. Sophie and Sarah got their heads together and arranged something else for the ladies.

The stag came around and was a knockout event. "What went on?" you ask. Well they did go to the agreed location, and they did go sea fishing, and they did…

Sorry, exactly what went on during the stag—must stay on the stag. Except what Connor decided to share in his speech.

Ashley arranged to have a final rehearsal of his speech with Reg the week after the stag and immediately leading up to the wedding. The best place to do it was in the barn at the hotel. This allowed him to get the feel of the location, so the following Saturday would not be so daunting. It would also give him a few days to recover from the stag do.

"Right, here we are, Reg. It was a cracking idea of yours to have the final rehearsal here. What do you think of the venue?"

"Yes, an ideal location. This barn is fantastic. You were right about it having the wow factor."

"That's what Sophie and I thought as soon as we walked through the door."

"It's ideal for today. It's all very well using your imagination, delivering your words in your bedroom in front of the mirror, but this is much better. More like the real thing. That said, you'll still need to use the visualisation technique to see the audience right here in front of you."

Ashley positioned himself, "As I know the exact layout of the tables, I'm able to stand in my position at the top table and speak from here to you."

"Marvellous. I'll act as the MC and introduce you while you're still seated. Remember The Six S's. You'll be on a bit of an emotional high on Saturday afternoon. Get into that mood now and imagine all the guests, your wife…"

Ashley interrupted him, "My wife. Yes, Sophie will be my wife by then. It's only a few days away. What a weird feeling."

"Yes, as I was saying, get into that passionate, emotional mood with your wife, both sets of parents, your family and friends. Do all the things we have spoken about over the weeks to prepare for it. Okay? Ready?"

"Yep! Ready. Think of it, Sophie, my wife, nearly there. How odd!"

Ashley found the précised speech document on his tablet and sat on a chair in the spot that he would speak from the following weekend. Imagination was certainly needed as the barn was not laid out as it would be on the big day.

Before Ashley began, Reg had one last thing to say, "As we have all this space I want you to make sure your eyes meet everyone in the room. Remember to pan around, covering each table. So rather than fixing your gaze on me standing still, I will move very slowly round the room to encourage you to look around. It will help you relax."

Ashley drew a couple of deep breaths, started The Six S's, and thought to himself, "Sit; stand slowly; a gentle, pleasant smile; stay silent and get everyone's attention; scan the room making some eye contact; get the tablet up, not too high, right; another deep breath and…"—An interruption! Shock all over his face, Ashley said, "What are you doing here?"

His future father-in-law was walking into the barn. Ashley and Reg were completely lost for words.

Howard spoke, "Err—sorry, you two. Have I interrupted something?"

In stunned silence, the other two looked at each other. All that preparation and anticipation! And then, an interruption. And not any old interruption, it was Howard. What on earth was he doing there?

Howard quietly said, "Hello. Err. Just having a look round. Don't have much to do this week. Gwen and I have taken a few days off before Saturday. She's busy doing other stuff. Thought I'd take a look around at what I'm paying for. Err... and... err... well... room's a bit empty, isn't it?"

A rather deflated Ashley needed to know more. He walked over to Howard and they shook hands. "Have you met Reg? He's been helping me with my speech ready for Saturday."

"Err. Nice to meet you Reg. People have been saying great things about you and those peas of yours. Yes, you know Gwen don't you?"

Reg seemed completely lost for words but managed "Likewise, and thanks! Yes, Gwen gets down the gardening club."

Ashley said, "We were just about to run through my words for Saturday. Probably the last opportunity to do it. The room was free, so we arranged with the management to use the barn for an hour."

Howard, in his usual quiet, uncomfortable and shy manner simply said, "Look I don't want to interrupt you any longer. I'll be off." He simply turned and walked out.

Ashley and Reg looked at each other again while Ashley posed a question, "What was that all about?"

"Search me, Ashley."

They walked to the door and pushed it back open. Howard was nowhere to be seen. They walked into the corridor leading to the main hotel building and saw nothing, nobody, Howard had gone. They went back into the room.

Ashley stood shaking his head, "Odd that. Everything we've done towards the wedding has been discussed, so we've all known exactly what everyone is doing. Didn't know he was coming here today. Now I think about it I had asked Sophie to tell her parents I was coming here today. Maybe she forgot."

Reg obviously did not want to discuss Howard's appearance any further and was in a hurry to move on. "We haven't got much more of that hour left, Ashley, and we need to run through your words—twice."

"Bit of a coincidence, that. You will recall it was you, last time, who interrupted my practice a few weeks ago. Oh well, let's get on."

Ashley shrugged, got back to sitting on the chair and, tablet in hand, went through the preparation again. Deep breath. Six S's. Delivering the words while Reg moved slowly around the room encouraging him to pan his gaze across every person on every table.

Pan

Eye contact must be used to everyone present. So pan the room with your eyes throughout the BBC. You are communicating with everyone present, not just one or two people. Include those who do not appear to be looking at you. Strange as it may seem, they will feel your eyes upon them. We do this in normal conversation, so make this a conversation with a larger group of individuals. When talking to large groups, some people are quite a distance away so the tip here is to look over to something on each of the distant tables and everyone on that table will think you are looking at them individually. As you look at the closer tables, your gaze will need to focus on individuals. Just hold that gaze for a moment and then move on to someone else. This has the effect of personalising the speech for each person instead of giving the impression that you are just going through the motions.

Some presenters find it difficult to make eye contact. If you struggle, keep trying. However, should it still not work for you, do not make direct eye contact; look at the bridge of the nose instead. Those far enough away will believe you are looking straight at their eyes. Slight nodding of the head and a gentle smile enhances the eye contact.

Ask yourself: Who did I look at? Did I look at people at the back of the room? Left side? Right side? Front? Were they looking at me? If not, why not? Was it my fault?

At the conclusion, Reg was delighted, "You should be very proud of that, Ashley. I'm quickly running through the peas in my head, and they were all there. What do you think?"

"Well, surprisingly, I enjoyed it. Really satisfied. To highlight a couple of the peas, I feel that your moving around did the job for me to encourage panning around. I was also making allowances for people to laugh and clap, so I made use of the pace and pause."

Reg had done a good job on Ashley. "I only want to mention a couple of bits. Yes, good eye contact around the room and I did notice you were not looking at me all the time. You had the confidence to look at the other end of the room from me. Good stuff. How about doing it again? This time using the props to help bring those stories more alive."

"Oh, you saw my cardboard box under the table then. I couldn't make up my mind whether to use them or not."

"You must rehearse fully. Yes, use them for the next run-through. Let's get straight on with it."

And they did it all again. This time, with the use of the items from the box.

At the end, Ashley was beside himself with excitement, "Absolutely loved it. Peas for breakfast, dinner and wedding speeches. I'm over the moon with that. Really pleased you encouraged me to bring and use my props. They made it even better."

"Ashley my friend, you are going to knock them dead at the weekend. Exceptional work."

"Thanks, Reg. It's been great working with you."

"The pleasure has been mine. Now, if it's okay with you, I'd like to settle down in the lounge with my laptop and do some other work."

"No problem at all. I've got to get back to the office."

They said their goodbyes and Ashley left the building while Reg made his way to the lounge area. As he walked through the car park, Ashley saw Howard's car but no sign of him. He thought, "That was odd. Him turning up like that and me not knowing anything about it. Sophie probably forgot to tell me." He headed back to work.

Only a few days later, Ashley Jamison and Sophie Williams became Mr and Mrs Jamison. It was a glorious day in more ways than one. The weather was warm and sunny, which was good for the whole event, especially the photographs.

So, let us now go back to where our story started.

You will recall the wedding party, and all the guests were in the hotel after the ceremony. They had started moving in the direction of the barn…

As everyone moved forward Sophie's Dad, Howard, at the front of the moving crowd, stopped.

Sophie was right behind him. "Dad, mind my dress! What are you doing?"

Howard stood on the bottom step of the staircase leading up to a side room. He gained everyone's attention by gently tapping a glass with a spoon. "Oops! Sorry, darling. Don't worry. Trust me."

Everyone was now facing Howard. Over ninety sets of eyes looking at him. He repositioned himself a little further up the stairs so that his head was just a bit above everyone else.

Sophie looked at her dad and spoke to Ashley, "His eyes are almost popping out of his head. He's terrified."

"This isn't like your dad. He said he wasn't going to give a speech. What on earth is he doing?"

He felt, looked and sounded worse than Connor. Just as he started to speak, Connor, who had come to a sudden halt shouted, "Oh, sugar."

Sophie who was right next to him, cried out, "Oh no, he's tripped over the bottom of his pea pod outfit."

Two of the peas fell off and rolled to the bottom of the staircase.

Someone shouted, "It's okay, I'll get them."

Nobody was prepared for what was to come next.

So what did come next?

Howard was as white as a sheet and looked like a deer caught in headlights. He sounded shaky, but spoke. "Folks. Some months ago I said there was no way I could, nor would, speak today. However, following some really fantastic help and support from a friend known as Reg the Veg, I have a bit of a surprise. No, I am still not going to speak." He nodded and pointed to the member of staff who had called everyone to order a few moments earlier.

A very proficient member of staff was performing the duties of MC (Reg wasn't officiating but both he and his wife were present), "Ladies and gentlemen, please turn slightly to your right. It will take just a few moments for the screen to come down. Sophie's dad has a super surprise for you all."

Sophie looked at Ashley then quite loudly and firmly said, "There you are, I knew he was up to something."

The screen descended, and a video appeared on it.

Howard was giving his father of the bride speech. Guided by Gwen, he had secretly been working with Reg and his peas, but even so, he could not bring himself to address everyone live. During the previous week, he met up with Reg who filmed the speech at the hotel, in the very barn where the wedding and reception were being held.

The speech received applause beyond belief. Tears! You have never seen tears like it. People regarded this as one of the biggest wedding surprises ever witnessed. A lot of backslapping took place. Then, as soon as Sophie mopped up her tears of joy she approached her dad, "Dad, you old fox, you! How did you pull that off?"

"With a lot of encouragement and support from your mum and even more help and patience by Reg. That guy is brilliant. That said, we nearly got caught the other day when I turned up at the hotel and bumped into Ashley when he was practising his speech with Reg in the barn. I mucked the time up and got there over an hour early."

Peas! Being prepared took on another meaning as Ashley and Gerry had to then adjust their speeches slightly to account for Howard's surprise. They acknowledged his speech at the outset of theirs.

So, what happened about Connor's fallen peas? Well, everyone was paying so much attention to Howard's on-screen performance that Connor got left out scampering about on the floor. He had to pick up his own peas and stick them back on. He was as amazed at Howard's speech as all the others, and thought, "How do I follow that?"

Then, everyone walked along the connecting walkway to the barn for the other speeches and the reception.

The speeches? They are coming. However, the epilogue is next—the conclusion to the story.

Reg's Podcast

"Remember, preparation is a long process. Be prepared for the unexpected. That reminds me of a line from Robert Burns, 'The best-laid plans of mice and men often go awry.' No matter how carefully a project is planned, something may still go wonky with it."

Chapter Eleven—Epilogue: The Passing Out Parade

As Reg outlined, every presentation or story (including this one) needs to have its Parthenon or BBC; beginning, body, conclusion. Here comes the conclusion.

So, how did it all go? What happened next? What is going on now?

As with any fairytale ending, everyone survived. All those involved are well and lived to tell their stories of success. There is a further surprise, however. The mums.

After all the planning, preparing and practising, all speakers were over the moon with their ultimate delivery efforts. Their excitement and pleasure were shared by friends and family. Many words of thanks and congratulations were offered. All the speakers had approached their speeches in different ways. Because of the effort put into the overall preparation and production, it was a highly successful and memorable event.

It is important to note that everything had been carefully arranged with the hotel wedding coordinator and the catering staff, so the timings had to be spot on. That said, there were surprises that needed to be handled as they arose.

As in our story, many people now dot their speeches about between the meal courses, while others prefer they be delivered after the starter so everyone can enjoy the meal without being stressed over what is to come. Nothing is set in stone. Whatever you decide to do, it is always essential to liaise with the staff at the wedding venue to ensure the overall timetable is agreed.

It is also acknowledged that some folks choose not to have speeches at all. It is very much a personal choice.

Remember that if people wish to speak during the ceremony, arrangements need to be made with the appropriate official, e.g. religious leader, registrar or celebrant.

So how did each perform?

Speakers at the Ceremony

Abbie and Toby read during the ceremony. Both were arranged by Sophie directly with the registrar and the hotel's wedding coordinator before the wedding.

Toby

Ashley's friend read his love story from an app on his mobile at the ceremony. His words were constructed with the assistance of a celebrant friend.

Fortunately, as a junior school teacher specialising in English and drama, coaching was not necessary.

Note that reciting or reading to yourself is one thing, but doing so reading to others is a skill in itself. That said, many of the skills are the same as those in Reg's pea pod, especially occasional eye contact (panning with the eyes over the book or script to the audience). An essential communication skill.

Abbie

Even though Sophie's friend, a history teacher at a senior school, was used to reading or reciting out loud to large groups, she had not done so at an event such as a wedding. It was an advantage that she lived quite close to Toby and, even better, that they were both in the same profession.

This meant they were able to work together preparing for their presentations and could draw on each other's delivery experience. Another key technique both used carefully was pace and pause, placing emphasis on words and phrases where and when necessary.

There is a need here to ensure the listeners hear every word—reading at an appropriate pace is crucial. She, like Toby, used her smartphone as an aide-mémoire when reciting her poem.

Sophie's intuition was correct, Toby and Abbie are now an item and, who knows? They may be speaking at their own wedding in the not too distant future.

Speakers at the Reception

Each appears here in the order that they spoke, which is not the way things had been planned.

H oward

Howard, as the father of the bride, would normally be responsible for the first speech and setting the scene for the other speakers. He became a special case in that he had never done anything like speaking to more than a small group of friends and was seriously concerned about speaking to a much larger group. He had openly discussed his anxiety about getting up to speak as well as letting his daughter and the wedding party down.

Anyway, Howard secretly worked through all the same theory with Reg as he did on an individual basis with Ashley. Howard created a full script without whittling it down into a précised format with just bullet points and tried very hard to overcome those common fears. He put into practice the techniques shared by Reg to handle his problems, but to no avail.

Now, if you believe that research about people being more willing to die rather than speak in public, how do you think some people might react when they find out they are to be videoed? So you can imagine Howard's reaction to the suggestion that he give the father-of-the-bride's warm-up speech by video at the outset of the reception. Something very effective and truly memorable. There is that word yet again—memorable. After all, how many weddings have you attended or heard of when a speech had been recorded and played to the guests?

It was all agreed, however, that the final filming would be recorded during the week before the wedding. Howard needed to be in his wedding outfit.

And so it was that, armed with his carefully crafted speech, a video star was born. That said, a number of practice runs were needed. After all, practice makes perfect. Howard's video was extremely well received.

Howard may not speak in public ever again, but his confidence was projected sky-high, as his quietly spoken voice was. He certainly projected this well.

Project

Adopt a conversational type of approach while speaking up and out so everyone can hear you. Make sure everyone can see and hear you. If necessary, stand on something. Project your voice and yourself—project your personality to every table and every guest, across the whole space. Many politicians and other speakers stand on something when addressing crowds out in the streets. Projecting elevates you above the audience. Some use a megaphone or sound system to ensure their voice is heard well. Some speakers stand on a chair to address the listeners. A bit of a gimmick, yes, but think how impactive this can be—everyone will remember the speaker. Vary the pitch and tone as much as possible to make the voice more interesting. Use a microphone with a sound system if necessary.

Ask yourself: How did I project myself and my voice? Could I be heard? Could I be seen by everyone? Was my voice varied? How do I know this?

G erry

Gerry was a different case. Now, here was someone with a fair amount of experience of public speaking, who felt confident enough to speak at the wedding. However, as he had never had any formal training in presentation skills, he had turned to Reg just to get some advice on the wording of his short script. In doing so, they inevitably got round to talking about some of the peas. Reg shared with him a copy of his fifteen peas. The pea for Parthenon was particularly useful as his original script lacked a sound structure. Once introduced, it became an effective BBC.

He is now mentally picturing the Parthenon whenever he creates a presentation for delivery at work.

A shley

So, was all the work carried out with Reg worth it? Here was an individual who had been required many years previously to present information to his fellow students at university. Since then, he had often shared information at work with a handful of his work colleagues. And that was the extent of his experience. No real standing at the front talking to large groups of individuals.

Having never been on a professional public speaking course, here was an opportunity to learn from someone with loads of experience who was willing to share his peas. There were times when he disagreed with Reg and even felt uncomfortable with some of the exercises but, yes, it was worth it. He was successful with his wedding speech and was then able to transfer all those newly-gained skills to future presentations at work. With his enhanced confidence, he is now able to use his personality to full effect. Who knows! Could he become an assistant to Reg?

Ashley continues as a solicitor with the same firm. However, he has become more qualified and is hoping to have a partnership offered to him in the near future.

S ophie

Sophie gathered ideas from Ashley as he talked about his coaching sessions with Reg. She knew that, traditionally, the bride did not usually get involved in speech-making, but in recent years more and more brides were saying, "It's my day so I'm going to jolly well have my say, too."

She was keeping the work with Ashley a secret from everyone else to surprise others at the wedding reception. Sophie was in a similar situation as her husband-to-be, in that the last time she had got up in front of a group of people to speak in a more formal setting was at university. She, like Ashley, recognised the usefulness of these techniques beyond the wedding and now uses them in her professional life. That is why she asked Ashley to pass details on to her. As well as keeping it secret from the rest of the wedding speakers, she intended her speech to be brief and to the point (KISS). She shared just a few emotional words of thanks to her parents especially, a passionate message for Ashley, and included a little story to make it memorable and personal.

Her short address to the guests was very simple but highly memorable, as she built compelling pictures through the story she told.

Sophie has now become self-employed as a personal trainer and is building her client base.

If you were hoping that tiny feet were on their way, you might be disappointed. As a couple, they are not in any hurry to enlarge their family just yet. Maybe in another year or so. That said, there is a little surprise awaiting you in Ashley's speech.

Sarah

The maid of honour and only bridesmaid did not give a speech as such. It was more of a simple thank you for the gift that the bride and groom had given her. There was also a quick mention of the initial meeting between Ashley and Sophie. She really did use KISS and used it to perfect effect, particularly with the brief reference to something that Sophie had done when young.

She and Sophie remain very good friends and will probably remain so forever.

Gwen and Penny

What about the mums? Well, they put their heads together and agreed that they did not want to seek Reg's guidance and reserved the right to speak or not, should they change their minds on the day of the wedding. The two plotted a plan and did not tell anyone about it. They came up with a fantastic idea. A double act of passion and humour made it a truly memorable performance.

Because they had not discussed their speech with anybody, it caused a bit of a problem with the timetabling. They thought their two-minute performance could be slipped in shortly after everyone had taken their seats, before the first course. Because this had not been arranged, they had to wait till just before Connor, and this did have an impact on his speech.

Their mini-performance was magnificent. They may not have had a starring role in the proceedings and may not receive repeat performance requests, but everyone enjoyed their efforts. Their mothering instincts and personalities shone through.

C onnor

Now, he was a completely different case. Connor was the sort of character who left things, well, everything, till the last minute. Oh! And this included organising the stag event. Although it was not Reg's business to interfere, he suggested to Ashley that Connor ought to be chased to ensure he had put something together in advance of the event, and that meant before the stag do in Barcelona. Any appropriate events occurring in Barcelona could soon be added later. Regardless of this, Connor chose to do it his way.

Many people believe that, because they are generally confident and talk to others regularly down the pub, they can also talk to a hundred or so people at a wedding. But, when that mass of eyes turns and faces them, and there is silence in the room, their confidence suddenly dies. Connor soon realised that preparation is key to all public speaking performances.

However, after all the dilly-dallying and the last-minute panicking by Connor, his efforts went down a storm. All the props he used during the speech really did bring his words to life, especially the thing at the back of the barn which he held back right till the conclusion of his speech. He followed the advice offered and did not tell any jokes, but he was quite engaging and mildly humorous. It was 'alright on the night.'

There was an unusual twist in his speech caused by the knock-on effect of un-timetabled speeches. Make sure you read them.

Having set up his own highly-successful plastering business employing others, he is now considering becoming a business start-up mentor for others wishing to do something similar. He has now hinted at an Ashley-type coaching period due to a business offer made to him by one of his major clients. He may, therefore, be sowing his own peas soon.

R^{eg}

Reg thoroughly enjoyed his work with Ashley and Howard, and continues to do so with others. Being retired, he loves pottering around in his garden, particularly when it comes to pea planting and seeing the result of his efforts. He is then able to use real peas when coaching his public speaking clients rather than just the pictures on the walls of his shed.

He continues to take clients on a journey from little knowledge and confidence to successfully delivering information to others publicly. Having worked so closely with speakers for this wedding, he now has a new group of friends who will no doubt be invited to his forthcoming wedding anniversary. Reg will not be leaving his speech till the last minute.

And Finally...

So successful was this wedding that those who witnessed it and the speeches, will still be talking about everything at Sophie and Ashley's silver wedding anniversary. Or, in Reg and his wife's case, their golden wedding anniversary.

You can download all the speeches and other useful resources at:
www.theweddingspeechcoach.com/bookspeeches.html

Acknowledgements

A All these people have had a hand in helping turning an idea in my head into this book.

Alison Coates, Alison Jones, Brian Wadman, Carole Spiers, Clare Concannon, Don Deacy, Glenda Shawley, John Constable, Keith Martin, Laurie Bernard, Les Ellis, Martyn Pentecost, Peter Oxley, Richard Hagen, Sarah Williams, Steve Preston, Sue Richardson, Suzy Pool and Terri Shanks.

There are so many others to be thanked who have influenced various aspects of this story and they possibly will never know it. They extend from family and friends to fellow professionals and clients.

Some aspects of the story are close to reality and therefore so are the characters. Some know who they are, while some will not. Others will know once they read this book.

Please forgive me if you have been inadvertently left off the list.

Thank you one and all.

About the Author

Thirty years as a police officer with the Metropolitan Police in London trained Graham Le-Gall in every aspect of soft skills. He had to communicate clearly, concisely and convincingly when dealing with members of the public in every imaginable situation.

He mentored and coached many recruits in communication skills within the police service. In the latter part of his police career he was selected to be one of the core management development trainers at the Met's Hendon Police College. As well as training recruits and senior officers in communication and leadership skills he was also responsible for training and coaching new trainers within the organisation.

Since establishing his own consultancy firm he has specialised in management development, soft skills subjects, training trainers and helping those who wish to develop public speaking and presentation skills. His academic qualifications (Graham is a qualified teacher, Home Office accredited trainer and has a Masters in Human Resource Management), combined with his varied and extensive experience, allow Graham to tailor his training to every individual and context for maximum results.

After experiencing the challenges of preparing his own father-of-the-bride speech he began to work, to great success, with others in developing and presenting their wedding speeches. From this experience this book was born...

Find out more at:

Other Books from mPowr Publishing

Your Slides Suck!
David Henson
ISBN—978-1-907282-78-2
The book for all speakers! How to make engaging, empowering and effective PowerPoint presentations.

Hire Power
John Wallace
ISBN—978-1-907282-83-6
For HR specialists and senior management. How to leverage strategic resourcing to create a competitive advantage.

Mission: Leadership
Lifting the Mask
Ben Morton
ISBN—978-1-907282-71-3
For mangers, coaches and leaders. How to create and support strong teams by encouraging heroes, liberating victims and challenging the villains in your workplace.

The Key:
To Business & Personal Success
Martyn Pentecost
ISBN—978-1-907282-17-1
For those who are passionate about growing and developing. How to discover yourself and the most effective ways for you to flourish and enjoy success.

The HR Warrior
Nicola Williamson
ISBN—978-1-907282-84-3
For those who want to put the human into HR... A revolutionary approach to all stages of recruitment, development, progression and exit.

The Publisher's Guide Series

The Heist:
Cracking the Marketing Code
ISBN—978-1-907282-24-9
For those who want to understand how to use books as a powerful element of their marketing mix. The key elements required for a powerful strategy.

Storyselling Your Business
ISBN—978-1-907282-59-1
For those who understand that stories are the most powerful tool for persuasion and promotion. Strategy, techniques and tactics that will revolutionise your marketing approach and your entire business.